Praise for *At Death*

"Most people know Frederick Marx from Hoop Dreams, Journey From Zanskar, and other fine films. They probably don't know that he is a longtime student of dharma, an ordained Zen priest, and a gifted writer exploring the terrain of the human heart. This book shivers with the frailties of what it means to be human, enfolding loss in all its forms, finding a way through acceptance and the pure ground of being back to love."

-Ram Dass, author of Be Here Now

"This book is one's man's story of love, loss, and realization; actually it is a story that many of us know or will know. Heartbreaking, beautiful, intimate, challenging ...this is a book we should all read."

-Rev. Joan Jiko Halifax

"Frederick Marx has written a touchingly intimate account of love, loss and healing. Losing a loved one is something most everyone faces at some point in life. At Death Do Us Part shows the possibility of navigating through this journey with consciousness, understanding and an open-heart."

-James Baraz, co-author of Awakening Joy: 10 Steps to Happiness; co-founding teacher Spirit Rock Meditation Center, Woodacre, California

"Raw and beautiful, this tender, joyous look into the shared intimacy of a mature couple, seems almost too secret to put into words. I felt touched so many times in so many ways by this unique wisdom-teaching. As I *slowly read the book, I kept falling in love with Frederick. His utterly fearless transparency constantly endeared him to me."*

—Bill Kauth, co-founder of The ManKind Project; co-author of A Circle of Men and We Need Each Other

"At Death Do Us Part is a book about life, of change, of opening your heart. Reading Frederick's words and mulling over his stories, I feel that my world is now filled with more depth and more flavors, as well as some new questions and insights about this thing we call being alive. A beautiful, moving book."

-Marc Lesser, author of Less: Accomplishing More By Doing Less

"I was deeply moved by Frederick's story beginning with the words from his introduction. 'How do you get over losing your life partner?' This is an experience none of us want to go through, yet it is one that is part of the inevitable human journey. Frederick offers us a glimpse into our present and future losses, but does it in such a beautiful and caring way, we feel like we're with a true guide and loving friend who is holding us in his kind embrace."

-Jed Diamond, author My Distant Dad: Healing the Family Father Wound

"How to express how deeply I am touched by this remark- able tale of the truth of living and dying? This is not just an autobiography and history of [their] time together and its cancerous ending, but also a Buddhist dharma teaching. Life and death lived within the Buddhist perspective. It is gift from them to and for all of us. We all need to come to

compassionate understanding and radical acceptance of the truth of dying. This book is a great sharing teaching of this understanding."

-JunPo Denis Kelly, Abbot of the Hollow
Bones Order of Rinzai Zen

"I have always been aware of Frederick's brilliance, so easy to see in his important documentaries. Now he takes that brilliance once again through the portals of his heart, to share a very intimate, soul-searching book of loss and grief...and beauty and love. All of which can be found in his cracked open heart upon the death of his wife."

-Meredith Little, author & founder
of School of Lost Borders

"It's surprisingly enjoyable, moving, captivating, engross-ing. Marx revives-reanimates-re-loves–his partner–not as saint, but as person–with textured, reverent, and humorous delight, showing that grief is not a one way trip to a lugubri-ous terminus but a single stop on a vast, circuitous journey, a dizzying, dazzling topography filled with aliveness, pres-ence, love."

-Jiwon Chung

"Just like Frederick I've been lost. Like him, Buddhist meditation changed my fundamental perspective on how to approach life, how to deal with failure. There's a level beyond understanding on offer here...Frederick knows that there's a time when being out of integrity, out of whole-ness, our internal sense of good, becomes too great a pain for a man to carry. Like other good men, he has that strong

internal compass to guide that pull back to being the man he knows he can be."

-Rich Tosi, co-founder of The ManKind Project; co-founder of A Couples Weekend

"At Death Do Us Part is a beautiful testament and memorial to an extraordinary woman through deep realizations of love and relationship. The experience of reading At Death Do Us Part reminds me of a Buddhist, "bare bones," practice of just showing up for what is, with no place to hide. This is not an easy read; yet, it is an important undertaking that evokes within the reader the courage that was necessary to share this narrative."

—Dr. Timothy P Dukes, author, The Present

Praise for *Rites to a Good Life*

The text is filled like a banquet with rituals, stories, medicines, quotes and models, recipes for genuine growth and transformation. This deep connection to the sacred, and to your own unique gifts and courageous place in the world is what Rites to a Good Life, and Rites of Passage reminds you is possible.

Rites to a Good Life is a call for us all to reflect on our own personal journey and its place in the culture and cosmos around us. It is not just for our youth. We need the gifts of these Rites at every stage of life and we need ways to continually renew our connection to our deepest purpose and the sacredness of life.

I hope this book inspires you to do so.
—Jack Kornfield, author and co-founder
of Spirit Rock Meditation Center

A powerful and visionary endeavor. Inspiring.
—Joan Halifax, author and founder Upaya Zen Center

The soothing balm we need in a world on fire. This is the handbook we all need to revive the hero within us with practical and accessible daily rituals for personal growth that just may transform your life and enable you to change those of others.
—Maryann Howland, author of Warrior Rising

Our world is always made easier by rites of passage, and it's made better by this book on the subject. This is a very fine book; thoughtful, well researched and well written.
—Curtis Mitchell

A fine and important book. The framework provided, the quotes from a range of people and cultures, and the personal story woven in will keep people well involved.
— Meredith Little, author of The Four Shields:
The Initiatory Seasons of Human Nature

"In Rites to a Good Life, Frederick Marx ministers to his readers by slowing them down enough to consider how to craft a life worth living in a hectic and traumatizing world. In so doing, he provides readers the tools to help bring transformation out of trauma, personal depth out of despair, and

a life of intentionality out of a life of superficiality. Books like this can recreate reader's worlds.

— Joel Edward Goza, author of America's Unholy Ghosts: the Racist Roots of Our Faith and Politics

Frederick lays out the mechanics of rites of passage in a clear and reasoned manner, allowing the reader to relate and make personal the benefits. More importantly, he demonstrates rites of passage are not a once in a lifetime event. Rites of passage represents a common human framework for change and growth repeated over the span of a lifetime. It seems the best strategy is to understand and become skillful. I enjoyed the read.

— Craig "Snake" Bloomstrand, author of Wise Men Look

In my years of doing Rites of Passage work with boys and young men, I've never met anyone with more experience, insight or passion about those issues than Frederick Marx. All of those qualities come through on virtually every page of this book. Frederick never fails to show respect toward those whose approach to rites of passage may vary from his own. ... In our culture that has lost the significance of mentoring for both girls and boys, it's the destructive impact we see every day from broken, wounded males that demands crucial attention. Frederick's life work, and this book, have the capacity to bring healing to those wounds.

— Craig Glass, author of Passage to Manhood: Field Guide

Turds of Wisdom

Other Works by Frederick Marx

At Death Do Us Part
Rites to a Good Life

Films by Frederick Marx

Veterans Journey Home (a five part series)

• Kalani's Story
• Leaving it on the Land
• Solutions
• On Black Mountain
• Ben's Story

Rites of Passage
The Tatanka Alliance
The World as it Could Be is Within Reach
All Must Be Documented!
Journey from Zanskar
Boys to Men?
The Unspoken
Joey Skaggs: Bullshit & Balls
A Hoop Dreams Reunion
Hoop Dreams
Higher Goals
Inside/Out
Hiding Out for Heaven
Dreams from China
House of UnAmerican Activities
Dream Documentary

Turds of Wisdom

■ ■ ■

Irreverent Real-Life Stories from a Buddhist Rebel

Frederick Marx

Waterside Productions

Cover design by Onur Giray

ISBN-13: 978-1-958848-66-1 print edition
ISBN-13: 978-1-958848-67-8 e-book edition

Waterside Productions
2055 Oxford Ave
Cardiff, CA 92007
www.waterside.com

Contents

Epigraph

What I usually do … is share notes of what's been happening. I always talk about myself it turns out. But those of you that know, know that it isn't really "me," it's "us," and I just use myself as a case study that I know better than everybody else's case study. Because what awes me is how parallel our journeys are and how much when I'm going through something and I think, "Boy, this is really leading-edge stuff," I meet somebody and they say, "Gee, that's just what's been happening to me."

Look at all the great saints. They're all as neurotic as anybody else. It's just that it's kind of irrelevant. And so you don't have to change your neuroses. You just stop identifying with them. And you just make friends with them and they come by for tea.

The soul comes to the incarnation to learn something. And you learn best by involving yourself in the game. Lovingly watching oneself. Humorously. Humor and love. Humor and love.

Ram Dass
Excerpts from the film *Becoming Nobody*

Preface

This book contains stories of two kinds—episodes from my personal life and mini-essays on particular topics of interest. Some are Buddhist-themed; some have nothing to do with Buddhism. Nothing is meant to be sequential, either chronologically or thematically. For those things, I recommend a good book.

In a recent discussion with some friends, I asked whether they thought they were low- or high-maintenance individuals. I describe myself as high-maintenance. My girlfriend replied, "Well, if that's true, you do so much of the maintenance yourself, it's as if you're a low-maintenance person."

That's what this book is about—being a high-maintenance person but doing a lot of the maintenance myself. What I describe in these pages is a high-maintenance person—neurotic, difficult, demanding, contradictory, and critical. What I also describe is how I've learned to manage those challenges: the daily strategies, the coping mechanisms, the insights, and hopefully, the humor I've found along the way that make it possible to carry on. And boy, do I carry on!

Introduction

Over the years, I've worked on a fiction script based on my travails in the film world. This is a draft of the very first scene of *Death: A Comedy.*

EXT. FOREST – DAY

JOEY walks in a deep wood. He stops by a tree, looks around to ensure he's alone, and takes off his day pack. He takes out a hand spade and begins digging a small hole. Then he takes out a photo of Mike Jones, his archenemy. He drops it in the hole and looks at it. Then he looks around. We go to a long shot.

He stands up, drops his pants, and then squats down to lean his butt over the hole. Sure enough, he starts to drop a turd. He readjusts his balance in order to hit the target. Bulls eye! He turns around and checks. Pure satisfaction. He starts to get up. But he loses his balance and puts a hand behind him for support. Right into the shit.

End Scene

My friend Sonika suggested I name this book *Chicken Shit for the Soul.* I found that hilarious and might've gone with it if I wasn't afraid it would invite some strongly worded letters from Jack Canfield's lawyers. I could well end up in serious legal jeopardy because my book in no way satirizes the Canfield brand. (Perhaps perversely, satires and parodies have better-protected legal standing than titles that appear to merely ride on someone's coattails.) Though I never read the original *Chicken Soup for the Soul* book, I suspect I would like it. My book might further the objective of the Canfield brand—spreading comfort and meaning. Can't do that!

For the longest time, my working title was *Turds of Meaning*. It makes no sense, really. I thought it was funny; it appealed to my love of absurdity. With Turds as the first word, the title should stand out prominently in any book listing and hopefully grab attention. I pictured a giant poop emoji as the cover—a smiling pile of shit—also drawing laughs and attention. Chocolate ice cream, anyone?

These days, the attention economy is decisive. With the glut of product out there in the infosphere—so much of it total shit (yet, unlike my book, not announcing itself as such)—it takes something bold to quickly grab attention. My secret hope is that this book, which is superficially only about laughs, will offer people a lot of meaning and perhaps even some wisdom on how to live a happier life with more ease and acceptance. It was also a hearty "fuck you!" to the mainstream publishing industry, which traditionally, would never publish a book with "turds" in the title.

Call it passive-aggressive, but I wanted revenge on the pooh-bahs who turned their backs on my first two books. I wanted to poke my finger right in the eye of those who deemed them unpublishable. One major publishing house told my book agent that he wouldn't hesitate to take my second book if only a Black writer had written it. Gee, I thought good ideas and good writing were good ideas and good writing regardless of who it came from. Not in today's world. Thank you, publishers. Let me drop some Turds of Meaning on you.

Most people laughed when they heard the title. Some people groaned. Others simply couldn't grasp it. They'd lean in and splutter, "What did you say?!" About a third of the book's advance readers insisted vehemently that the book should be renamed. Worse, they felt that the book wasn't all that funny. Back to the editing room!

Does the world need another Buddhist book? Possibly. But no one's looking to me to write it. As I neared publication, John Hlinko suggested riffing on well-known Buddhist phrases and maxims. I had a lot of fun concocting all kinds of nonsense titles springing off that idea. Unfortunately, *The Jew in the Lotus* was already taken. That led me to a trial run with *EnLighten Up!* It captured the humorous intent along with the Buddhist theme. But it made the subtitle redundant.

I was challenged by my editor to return to *Turds of Meaning.* (Thank you, Ryan!) My scatological predisposition was happily maintained alongside my love of the outrageous. Am I alone in thinking the sacred and the profane exist in close proximity? Only at the eleventh hour did I shift to *Turds of Wisdom.* (Thank you, Austin!) The play on words with "words" is good. The "words/turds" rhyme is funny but subtle, and "wisdom" makes more sense than "meaning." I lost the complete absurdity factor, but it's close in humorous impact.

Here's the reject list. Imagine encountering these titles at your favorite bookstore:

- *We Become What We Think. Stop Thinking That Shit!*
- *Impermanence ... Where Was I?*

- *They Say That Waking Up Is Hard to Do ...*
- *Attachment Leads to Suffering. Get Away from Me!*
- *Ennervana*
- *Letting Go, Letting God, Letting Goddamn!*
- *Karma, Shawarma*
- *Awakening Under the Booty Tree*

Introduction 2

It's untrue that there's nothing funny about trying to be funny. It's hilarious. All that yearning and effort, that sweat and ache … that in itself is funny. Serious things *are* funny. Since I'm so serious all the time, I should be a laugh riot.

A cycle of revelation and obliviousness has followed me throughout my life. When I'm having what seems like a big revelation or a cathartic epiphany, to those around me, I'm feverishly underscoring my obliviousness. They knew it all along but were too kind to let me know.

The closest I came to stand-up comedy was a very informal comedy performance troupe I joined in college. It was so informal I don't think we had a name. We performed two or three times in a basement coffee house for about forty of our friends. Our signature song was "Day-Old Bread" sung to the tune of "Day-O (The Banana Boat Song)." It was a tribute to the cheap, day-old bread sold at our favorite late-night coffeehouse. "Day! It's a day, it's a day old. Day-old bread cost fifty cents less. … It don't taste bad, it's not stale or smelly …"

Somehow, I thought that if I just took off my clothes, I'd be hilarious. Accordingly, the reviewer at the student newspaper commented that the one skit in which I did not take my clothes off was actually funny. This set the tone for much of my future in comedy. When I tried to be funny, I usually failed. When I was serious and trying to be sincere, people would laugh. Telling people I planned to write a comedy book usually launched them into hysterical fits. I was off to a good start.

I have to laugh; my life depends on it. Not like Norman Cousins because of cancer, laughing himself into wellness. My quick intolerance for injustice, coupled with my reflexive worldview of victim, doused with impatience regarding all forms of incompetence, inefficiency, and lack of accountability, make for a potentially toxic combination. Though it would happen quite regularly, I used to say, "I'm just angry." Now I call myself a curmudgeon. A comical perspective on events is the one strategy that might pull me through the coming collapse of modern industrial civilization. Trust me, it's coming. We might as well have a good laugh about it. I am Jewish after all.

Both sides of my family were one hundred percent Ashkenazi. My father was a German Jew and my mother a Russian Jew. Where in that equation do you commonly find the expression "happy-go-lucky"? Maybe it's genetic. I carried a world of hurt and victimization long before I knew the word Weltschmerz. When I was in my teens and twenties, I used to tell myself I was carefree and easygoing. Wrong! I was intense and self-deluded. I consider it one of the great achievements of my life that I'm now actually happy much of the time. Humor helps.

I've always loved comedy. In my student days, I thought Charlie Chaplin was the greatest cinematic genius to ever walk the planet, closely followed by Buster Keaton. To this day, I want to lie and say I'm related to the Marx Brothers. Groucho's *You Bet Your Life* was one of the best shows ever put on television. I tell people I'm his spiritual descendant. The great Jewish comics were some of my greatest heroes: Lenny Bruce, Peter Sellers, Don Rickles, Jack Benny, Albert Brooks, Rodney Dangerfield, Carol Burnett, Mort Sahl, Henny Youngman, and my beloved friend and mentor, Harold Ramis. One of my prized childhood possessions was a *Peanuts* comic book (I owned over twenty) that actor Jonathan Winters—a true comic genius—signed when nothing else was at hand for him to autograph. I remember his warm chuckle when I handed him the book. I'm not sure how I also didn't have one of my beloved MAD magazines on hand. One wedding vow I made to my late wife was to make her laugh at least once a day. Though she's gone, I'm still trying to make *somebody* laugh.

My biggest intentional comedic success is probably my film *Hiding Out for Heaven*. The programming director of the 1990 NY Film Festival, Richard Pena, said it was the audience's favorite short film. Scenes for the TV Special *Higher Goals* that I directed and co-wrote with Tim Meadows of 1990s Saturday Night Live fame don't make people laugh but they do make them smile. If this book does nothing more, I can live with that, you grim-faced bastards!

As I was working on a feature film script in 1995, my girlfriend noted how much she liked coming home after work. "Now that you're writing a comedy, you're always in a good mood." The writing of this book is born from that awareness. Laughter does more than improve my demeanor. It gives me reason to live. If you do laugh or smile reading this book, I'm gratified. Just know that you came second. I wrote it in self-defense—protection from a fucked-up world. Isn't this what comics do? Who said keeping yourself amused is not a matter of life and death?

When I was nine, I thought if I inverted traditional structural patterns of humor, I could be really funny. What this meant practically was that I would speak sarcastically every time I was serious and vice versa. I thought I was a genius. I somehow missed observing how this was the standard operating procedure for every nine-year-old. That set the pattern for much subsequent humor throughout my life: completely mistaking when I was funny for when I wasn't. To this day, communication is interesting, if problematic, when I say things meant with absolute sincerity in the tone of a big joke. People get confused or pissed off. The reverse, as we know, can be hilarious. We call this dry humor. But if people don't figure out that you're joking, it can mean trouble. Nothing kills humor delivered with a straight face more than having to follow it up with "I'm kidding."

Once, I was quite the card. I find numerous comments from class-mates in my seventh-grade yearbook saying, "You should be in comedy." Surveying my eighth-grade yearbook, I see four that say, "You are a real nut." It's unclear whether this was meant in a colloquial way referring to my comic potential or whether they thought I needed urgent psychiatric care.

Making people laugh was just who I was. Was I covering my fears and insecurities with comedy? Keeping people at arm's length, simultaneously fearing and desiring intimacy while trying to control them with humor? Of course! And your point would be? Isn't that pretty much what every comic does in their formative years?

Despite my natural disposition for mocking myself and others, for irreverence, surrealism, absurdism, parody, satire, irony, sarcasm, and pretty much all forms of humor, I developed a reputation as a "serious" filmmaker, maybe even self-serious. Most people think of me as a somber guy. In case you missed it, my first book is called *At Death Do Us Part*. How did this happen? How did I get here?!

Did I miss my life's true calling to become a comic? Nothing fills me with more delight than making large groups of people laugh. Perhaps that accounts for all the humiliating gaffes I've made in public speeches. It is, of course, better to make people laugh intentionally, but I'll take what I can get. Perhaps I took a wrong turn somewhere and became better adjusted, less fearful, and insecure. Perhaps success as a serious filmmaker stopped me from yearning for praise—needing to win people's love through laughter. Fortunately, many subsequent years of failure have returned me to the source. To spend my final years making people laugh is now my highest aspiration. I've just got to finish one last film on death and dying first.

Photo by Carole Dyal

Childhood Romance

I don't know how common it is to be horny as an eleven-year-old in sixth grade, but I sure was. Or maybe it wasn't horniness, but love-sickness? At that age, discerning longing from libido and love from lust might be impossible. I had crushes on girls starting in third or fourth grade. In sixth grade, it suddenly seemed acceptable to act on them. I didn't know exactly what I wanted to do with girls, but I sure knew I wanted to do something.

During that year's study module on the human body, I recall some rudimentary instruction on what it is people actually do. Sex! The birds and the bees! "Pay attention children, this lesson won't be repeated!" Too bad for me. I needed a review. I still do. Due to undiagnosed ADD, a wandering mind, or incapacitating fear, I didn't absorb much. The only light bulb that went off in my head was the one blinking "potential hilarity." Though I knew nothing about sex, I knew it was a subject people made lots of jokes about. I was searching for an opening to crack wise. Finding one didn't take long.

"How come boys can't have babies too?" I asked, feigning, or perhaps attempting to feign, complete obliviousness. The class broke up in howls of laughter. I got the response I wanted. No doubt some of it was derision. But I had already learned the first commandment of stand-up comedy: any laugh is a good laugh. I was not above playing the fool. It's a strategy that has served me well throughout most of my life. I was seen and acknowledged, especially by the girls. The teacher took pains to give my question absolute respect, all of it undue. She answered thoroughly. I don't remember a single thing she said. I was busy basking in the attention.

One day a gaggle of girls appeared at my desk. "Do you like Lindsey?" No doubt flushing crimson, I did my best to play it cool. "Yeah, I like Lindsey." The gaggle shuffled back across the room to Lindsey. Picturing geese is fine, but I witnessed more of a centipede with four heads. There was some urgent conversation, whispering, and nervous laughter, then the gaggle shuffled back to me. "OK. Now you're going together. Meet her at the ice rink Saturday morning." The centipede shuffled back to Lindsey, laughed some more, and dissolved into four distinct creatures.

It was rumored that Gene Bennett had already gotten to third base with Lindsey behind the bushes in the schoolyard. Even though I didn't know what sex was or how exactly to accomplish it, I was familiar with third base. At least I thought I was. But maybe not. More likely I had to ask someone what it meant. Probably Bill Werstler.

During a sleepover that year, I asked Bill how babies were made. He was shocked that I didn't already know. What could I say? In school, I was too focused on getting laughs. Plus, my father was long dead and my mother didn't have the nerve to have that conversation. I was convinced babies came from kissing because in the movies they always cut from the couple's first impassioned kiss to pushing the baby in the pram. Bill laughed his head off at that one. Or maybe they came from intense affection. Or singing. I still remember the intense longing Andy Williams and Sandra Dee shared in singing "We're almost there!" during the forgettable film *I'd Rather Be Rich*. It didn't teach me squat about sex, but it probably started my lifelong obsession with blonds.

I should have had the good sense to retain Bill as a life coach. I could have used his services some years later to explain nocturnal emissions. By the time I was fifteen, wet dreams arrived with startling frequency. I thought I was peeing the bed. I would wake from a dead sleep, ejaculating. I would clamp down vigorously on my penis to stem the tide, desperate to stop my unforgivable transgression. How could I be fifteen and still pee the bed?! I was ashamed. As luck would have it, cutting off the firehose was easy because I always woke up with my hand on my penis. It took me years to understand this was no mere coincidence.

But Lindsey, now there was a real woman. Gorgeous. OK, she was twelve, but I was excited. I was also scared shitless. I consulted Jay Hashbarger—the man-boy who clearly was the biggest "playa" in the class. "What do you do with a girl when you're together?" His answer was unequivocal. "Buy 'em stuff." "There it is," I thought, "simple, plain, direct, easy. Truth from the elders." I had my answer. But I inquired further. "What can you buy them at the ice rink?" He answered with the world's most important four-letter word: food.

There it was. The mystery of the universe laid bare. That was something I could understand. It was a simple transaction. If I bought her food, I got to hold her hand. Maybe if I bought her a lot of food, I could kiss her. That made sense to me. I was always hungry. Though never "food insecure" in the sense the term is used today, I was always insecure about food—"When will I eat? When will I eat after that? Is there enough? Can I eat as much as I want? Or is that too impolite?" Trying to raise three kids while studying for degrees in higher education didn't afford my mother much time to consistently buy and prepare food. I never tried paint chips, but I might have if there were any available at home. Leaded, unleaded, who cares? Many a night my mother would rush home after six o'clock, talk me off the proverbial wall of hunger, and say, "C'mon, we're going to McDonald's." She knew that two Big Macs, large french fries, and a milkshake would hold me for a few hours. (What a carb load! Did anyone say "pre-diabetes?") Better still were all-you-can-eat restaurants. Pull your son up to the feeding trough, unharness him, and let him hoover up the slop. On Sundays, she would often drive us one hundred and fifty miles round trip to reach the Holy Grail of the nearest buffet.

The ice rink was the cool place to be for the cool kids on Saturday morning. I could skate well enough. But there was a problem. I didn't have skates. I knew I could rent them, but that was uncool. I had to buy speed skates; they were cool. But time was short. Neither Penneys nor Sears nor Kmart had speed skates my size. All we could find were figure skates. Figure skates? No man-child of John Wayne would ever be caught dead in a pair of figure skates! I was desperate. What was least-worse: figure skates or hockey rentals? There was no handbook on sixth-grade coolness to consult. Disconsolate, I took the skates. Well, my mother did; she paid for them. At least they were black. I don't think she ever knew how important they were to me, my ticket to the first date of my life. I wore them once. Children, tell your parents—hockey skates are definitely the way to go. Preferably as rentals.

That morning with Lindsey, I didn't know what to say or do. Of course, we arrived late. Dependent on my mother for rides, I was always late for everything. After my ashamed apologies, we skated around in silence. Did I say that she liked me because I was funny? Not only was I not funny, I could barely choke a word out from under my soldered lips. "Aren't you going to hold my hand?" she asked. "Yes, of course," I stammered. To this day, I still have to be told when and how to make the first move. Not only did I not attend the Cool Guy Making the Moves Finishing School, I was raised by a feminist mother. I knew by the age of ten that it was potentially offensive to put the moves on a girl. Yes, in 1966! Foreshadowing #METOO reaches back that far. I was too afraid.

Skating, skating, round and round we went. Auditioning for a cry-onic future, I would have been livelier frozen solid at -155°C with a popsicle stick up my ass. Sure, I had a reputation as a wise guy—always making jokes. I wanted to entertain her, make her laugh, see her sweet smile, and have her turn her bright eyes of blue on me. But I was terrified. "Are you hungry? Do you want something to eat?" That was all I could manage to say. The big money I saved up—perhaps five dollars in case she wanted a hot dog with all the trim-mings, fries, and a Coke—was burning a hole in my pocket. Finally, she said, "Look, I'll let you know if I get hungry, OK!" I think Dante had something else in mind when he described the rings of hell, but I felt like I was mapping them out on skates that day.

Back in class on Monday morning, I was told by the girls that I was no longer going with Lindsay. Mired in shame, I never went back to the ice rink again. For years, those skates sat in the closet gathering dust. Somehow, that early implosion set the pattern for relations with girls for years to come.

I didn't fare much better with Kay Kolkhorst. Later that year, when a different group of girls told me I was now going with her, I immediately sought out the advice of a different friend, Max Henson. At least I had the sense not to go back to Jay. "Buy her a ring," he said. "You blew it with Lindsey." Sigh. Maybe I offered to buy her the wrong thing?

At that time, the common practice was for the boy to buy the girl a ring to announce to the world, (i.e., your fellow classmates), you were now "going together." "Going steady" was the official term. Even at eleven years of age, that struck me as a really stupid idea. I thought, "I don't want to marry her. I just want to hold her hand and maybe, eventually, summon the courage to kiss her." The rings were cheap, of course; we weren't talking about diamonds. But five dollars for a plastic ring? Why bother? I guess the concept of dating was too sophisticated for my infertile mind.

So, I balked. Truth be told, I wasn't really attracted to Kay. She was wild and crazy, which I appreciated. No doubt estrogen was burning new rivers of lava in her brain no less than testosterone was in mine. Though I appreciated her sense of humor, I just didn't know what else to say when the girls came over to my desk. I didn't want to hurt her feelings. But no, I wasn't buying her a ring.

At the year-end class party, I hurt her feelings further. I danced with another girl, Cathy Caple. I thought, "You know, Cathy's kind of cute." I liked dancing with her. More to the point, *she* asked *me* to dance. The truth was I was too afraid to go up to Kay and ask her. Then I'd have to talk to her. I knew from experience not to do that. Not again. Please, god. Skating, dancing… being violently shy is an injury that has unlimited potential for harm. Later, on her way out the door, Kay stepped in front of me. With genuine hurt and outrage, through clenched teeth, she spit out, "You two-timer!" I was ashamed. I felt sorry for her. I wasn't proud of myself for hurting her feelings. But shame and awkwardness alone did not account for my out-of-place smile. For one thing, "two-timer" was a word only grown-ups used. Two-timing was light-years beyond me. I had yet to achieve any dating momentum whatsoever. I thought, "Honey, I could only wish. Maybe someday I'll be lucky enough to have a single girlfriend. Please, god, let me be a one-timer!" To get to the point where I might actually cheat on a girlfriend was beyond anything I could possibly imagine.

The obligatory Monday morning visit to my desk from Kay's girl-friends was deemed unnecessary.

I blew an opportunity to lose my virginity with a beautiful German girl when I was fifteen. By late winter in 1971, my mother had seen enough of us in our cramped two-bedroom apartment in Freiburg to send us packing for a week's ski lessons in the Schwarzwald. A girl the same age as me from northern Germany was on her winter break and joined us on the slopes. We spent much of the week cracking wise and making eyes at each other. Until that point in my life, I still hadn't even kissed a girl. In keeping with my string of sixth-grade debacles, shyness entombed me through the intervening years. I had crushes, violent ones, but I seemed destined for a life of celibacy.

The end of the week finally came and we crammed into a *bier-stube*. The ski instructor was making a play for her, which caught me off guard. Still, I did my best to play it cool and not let on that I was jealous. Later, headed to the hall for dinner and the evening party, we fell into walking together. Clearly, what I thought was well hidden behind a wall of cerebellum was written all over my face. She wasted no time in telling me outright that she wasn't really interested in the ski instructor. She might well have said, "Look, I've got a crush on you too." This was good because as soon as the words left her mouth and

I felt relief flooding through my body, I heard my mother's sharp voice saying, "Fred, get over here!"

Leaving my rising nerve melting on the sidewalk in the dirty snow, I bid my infatuation a hasty farewell and walked over to my mom. To say that I had totally forgotten about my mom would have been a gross understatement. To say that I didn't want to leave this girl's side would have been an even grosser understatement. If I had the nerve—admittedly, something in perpetually short supply—I would've grabbed her hand, fixed her with my eyes, and said, "Let's walk to France together and sleep in caves."

My mother was apoplectic. That morning, unable to reach her by phone, my older sister and I sent our ten-year-old brother, Larry, on the bus to go to Freiburg to find her. The farm family that was boarding us had been making noises about money, implying that they hadn't been fully paid for the entire week. We didn't know the details of the financial arrangements, and since neither Ellen nor I wanted to give up our time on the slopes, we made Larry go home to get it resolved. Always pick on the youngest. Sure, he was ten, but he had a streetcar pass and knew his way home from the bus station. I'd been waiting all week for the chance to be with my heartthrob and I wasn't about to give that up. She even had her own hotel room! I don't know what Ellen's excuse was other than she couldn't be bothered. Maybe she had a crush on the ski instructor. In my hormonal haze, I had completely forgotten about Larry.

My mother blasted me. She then marched my sister and I back to our farmhouse digs and blasted our hosts, saying she paid everything to the travel agency in advance and they should've been compensated by them. If not, it wasn't her problem. She then scolded us again for the twin transgressions of being irresponsible and sending Larry off to do the dirty work. Then she got back in the car and drove herself and my brother back to Freiburg.

Party, anyone? I was no longer in the mood, but I knew all too well that this was my last chance. Tomorrow we'd all be headed home. My sister and I rejoined the group. I'd lost any chance of a seat next to my girl and found the ski instructor's arm draped around her shoulders. Drinks, anyone? I drank and ate and grew more and more morose. I love dancing, but wouldn't ask her to dance. I love staring into beautiful female faces, but wouldn't move to talk with her. Instead, I watched the evening unfold like a slow-motion disemboweling of a goat. I was the goat. Darkness came and took me, throwing me under a slow bus with an uncertain driver. Back and forth my insecurities drove, grinding my hopes into wet asphalt.

It was one of the worst things that never happened to me. It was the first time I can recall becoming completely aware of my own willpower to self-destruct. Nuclear power. At first, she would look at me encouragingly, then with confusion, and finally with resignation. I told myself all kinds of lies to accommodate my inaction. "She doesn't really like me. She really wants the ski instructor. Look, she's laughing with him now!" I smoldered. I seethed. I sulked. "Why doesn't she come over and talk to me?" I thought every conceivable thought I could to wall myself off from facing my own inaction, my own cowardice. This wasn't mere insecurity. I willed myself into a state of complete misery. I drove a missile into the heart of my own darkness and imploded.

I never saw her again. Having taken the morning bus, she never joined us for the final morning on the slopes. In the perfect coup de grâce, the ski instructor bragged to us how they had been up all night fucking. He crowed about how incredible she was in bed. I never doubted it. I added downhill skiing to the growing list of activities (like ice skating) I'll never do again. What the hell is it with me and women and winter sports?

Bachelorhood 101

In the wake of my late wife dying, it shocked me just how quickly I reverted back to the old household management techniques of my bachelorhood. The closer you get to your seventies, the more essential these activities become. In the kitchen:

- Always cook everything in one pot. If something you want to make requires multiple pots or pans, make something else.
- Eat out of that pot. Putting food on a plate is wasteful—an unnecessary extravagance. Why wash an extra plate?
- If you do end up using a plate, always lick it clean. Just think of all the added nutrients and calories you'll get. You'll make washing easier and use less water. Plus, you'll be well-rehearsed for camping in the backcountry. The tongue exercise will keep it well-toned and prepared for your girlfriend. Once you cross a certain familiarity threshold, you can lick her plate too.
- Always eat with the same utensil you just cooked with.
- Always use the same glass—day after day, drink after drink. Just rinse it out when needed.
- Prepare meals by the expiration date. Eat whatever's oldest and needs to be eaten before it goes bad. If it's already gone bad, eat it anyway. Remember: what doesn't kill you makes you stronger! (The time to try to impress your new girlfriend that you have an iron stomach and can eat anything—old chicken, fuzzy cheese, spoiled milk, brown mayonnaise, rancid sunflower seeds, soggy mixed greens, etc.—comes later.)

- Remember: for breakfast, lunch, or dinner, a bowl of cereal or a peanut butter and jelly sandwich is nutritious and easy.
- Whenever you have guests over, quickly abandon this entire system or risk losing friends.

When your new girlfriend comes over:

- Buy fresh lettuce.
- Buy vegetables. Lots of them.
- Take out the garbage.
- Get higher-priced wine.
- Throw out all the dead and dying foods in the fridge.
- Make an elaborate meal using every pot and utensil you have. Fool her into thinking you cook like this all the time. Later, when your relationship is well established, revert to your bachelor ways. Tell her it just seems more practical to do everything that way. Never tell her the truth.

In the bathroom:

- Clean as you go.
- Splash a little water on every water- and spit-stained surface—faucets, handles, mirrors, and counters—while you're already brushing your teeth. Use your hand to wipe it down. Never waste paper towels or toilet paper.

When your girlfriend comes over, hide:

- Your anti-grinding teeth protector.
- Your hemorrhoid cream.
- Your toe fungus ointments.
- Your laxatives.
- Old porn magazines.

- Anal lubricants.
- Cheap, waxy toilet paper that might actually cut her. Get the soft stuff. Go triple ply.
- Encouraging messages from Mom taped to the mirror.
- The safety manual for "what to do in case of a heart attack."
- Your list of "people I'd like to see dead."

In your office, when your girlfriend comes over:

- Hide your recent bank statements.
- File away all the cease-and-desist letters from lawyers.
- Make sure your last will and testament isn't laying around.
- Put the books you've written, films you've made, and trophies, awards, and diplomas you've earned in clear sight near your desk.
- Hide all the photos of every dead person you know—your dead dog, your mom, your greatest benefactor and teacher—the entire gallery of all those passed. Don't remind her you'll be next!
- Put throw blankets over your erotic sculptures.
- Wash the windows so light actually gets through.

Changing clothes:

- Do it only when necessary. For example, when you're going to see the same people for the second day in a row.
- Rather than put that dirty T-shirt or socks or underwear in the laundry bin, take the ones you've been using for working out and wash those. Then move the original dirty ensemble to the workout bag.
- Every time your girlfriend comes over, change your clothes. Always wear your best-pressed shirts. Then, after she's been over a lot, start to wear your more faded jeans and shirts,

especially the ones with holes. Let her know that you've forgotten how to sew and that you value conservation. If she starts buying you nice clothes, marry her.

Cleaning the house:

- Hire cleaners. I don't care how low your income is, you can afford it.
- Whenever your girlfriend comes over, make sure the cleaners were there the day before.

Slowly, when the opportunities arise, start to point out all the broken and defective objects you have and suggest that they'd get fixed if only there were a real man around the house. If your girlfriend is handy with a screwdriver and a wrench, you've hit the jackpot. Propose.

If you have a spare bedroom, parking space, couch, or floor space, rent it out. You may have some explaining to do when the landlord pops over and sees eight people enjoying breakfast in your living room, but the passive income will help prepare you for a future of receiving social security.

No Self, No Problem!

"Enlightenment, don't know what it is," Van Morrison sings. Maybe not. But I have spent a good number of my waking days imagining that I know. Like most experiences I've never had, I always thought I could think my way to it. I've certainly had numerous, different, what I would call "openings," especially on meditation retreats. In one, I saw myself hovering far above the meditation hall, quietly surveying all in my purview—the deep redwood siding of the center's shaded buildings, the gentle surrounding hills, the low whistle of the wind, and bird calls from far away. I was this expansion. All I could see and hear and feel—this was the extent of my self, my being. A "field of awareness," as my teachers say. No more, no less. And there was a lightness in this knowing, a tremendous breadth.

I've also had numerous dramatic heart openings where I would simply weep at the holy magnificence of life. A blade of grass. A caterpillar. A caterpillar eating a blade of grass. A caterpillar eating the base of the blade of grass he's standing on. I've spent parts of whole days in this state. I wouldn't call it bliss. It can be a bit painful, actually. There's so much splendor that it becomes too much. There's so much to be grateful for that it's overwhelming. I do recommend it, just not for too long.

Out beyond ideas of wrongdoing and rightdoing, there is a field. I'll meet you there.
When the soul lies down in that grass, the world is too full to talk about.

Ideas, language, even the phrase 'each other' doesn't make any sense. *Rumi. [Translation by Coleman Barks]*

I also had what Buddhists like to call an experience of "*anatta*"—no self. Where even the phrase "each other" makes no sense. That was fun. During a week-long Zen *sesshin*, my teacher wanted the screen door to the meditation hall left open because "mosquitos were never present during the day." He was outside sitting under a tree, holding *dokusan*—a meeting with yogis—giving advice, encouragement, and teachings. It was a cool sunny day and he preferred being outside.

Us grunts were meditating indoors with straight backs, erect heads, and open eyes. Two half circles, facing each other in our formal Zen robes. Seventeen men in all. Silently praying that mosquitos wouldn't attack.

There is no hell quite like the hell of sitting in meditation and having a mosquito buzzing around you. I've always hated mosquitoes. I used to call out to my mother at night to come kill the bastards. Bless her memory, she used to come into the bedroom I shared with my brother, turn on the light and sit, tired, waiting patiently for the offender to land. She'd scan the walls, as would we. If we found it, she'd whack it with a rolled-up newspaper. I never fell asleep again with quite the same level of security, knowing the offender was handled, not unlike how Captain Willard handled Colonel Kurtz in *Apocalypse Now*! "Terminate … with extreme prejudice."

What is it with those little fuckers? Why do they always buzz around your ears? "I'm coming for you man!" Does that make it a fair fight in their eyes? "Don't say you weren't warned!" Targeting them, I've gotten bruises from hitting myself in the head. While camping, I've perfected the art of submerging my head and face using my sleeping bag and loose clothes, leaving only the tiniest of blowholes. Unfortunately, being ninety-nine percent sealed and fearing asphyxiation is a neurosis right up there with mosquitos and doesn't help with sleep.

When I was twenty-seven and living in China, I had to deal with the bastards again. When the mosquito netting around my bed failed, I sat up to wait it out. I ended up writing a short story called *The American Teacher and the Chinese Mosquito*. I passed off its simplicity by saying it was for kids, dedicating it to my newly found six-year-old Canadian friend Ezra.

My teacher, Junpo, loved to reenact a story about a meditation session in India when a mosquito landed on his nose. With semi-crossed eyes, he watched closely as she scoured the landscape, extending her proboscis to saw into his flesh, sniffing out a vein with her six needles, suctioning up the blood like a straw, filling her sac while excreting excess water, then leaving her parting gift of itch-invoking chemicals and potentially virus-laden saliva and flying off, drunk. He observed all this dispassionately, like a scientist. "What's the big deal?"

I spent the better part of one thirty-minute meditation period alternately cursing my fate and cursing him. When the bell rang and it was time for walking meditation, I closed the screen door to stem the flow of mosquitoes into the hall. I thought about how I would defend myself for this subversion. It clearly was the "right" decision to make, but so what? I found myself caught again in a tendency of mind I call "defending my life." I'm sure you know this one. Whatever action I take (or don't take), I'll spin out dozens of impassioned versions of defense. "But Your Honor, I was nowhere *near* the scene!" Say what you will about a childhood spent afraid of getting in trouble, I have the adult mind of a defense lawyer.

I imagined slapping a mosquito in the next meditation session. Movement of any kind is the ultimate no-no during *zazen*. "You'll violate decorum! Worse, you'll disturb the others," one part of me said. "Fuck it, who cares?" said the other part. I could imagine Junpo saying, "Who's the mosquito now? Who's the buzzing little irritant?" I imagined him changing my sacred *dharma* name to Little Buzz Kill.

And then it hit me, "Well, what if he does admonish me? What difference does it make? Eventually, we'll work it through and there will be peace." If he gets mad, doesn't get mad, what possible difference should it make to me? I can't retroactively change my behavior. I was taking a simple action, doing what I thought best. The rest is immaterial. Who gives a shit? I grew giddy. I started giggling. "There's nothing I can possibly do to alter the arising of subsequent events. So, relax, dude." And I did. I realized all I could ever do was use my best judgment to do my best, relax, and see what happens next.

I grew light. My body somehow became evanescent; it didn't matter what happened to it, to me. What could possibly happen that would make a difference? I experienced equanimity that was boundless. I felt like the air, unflappable. How can the wind disturb itself?

The bell rang and we hustled back to our sitting postures. A huge shit-eating grin blew across my face. I sat. I breathed. I thought, "What's the difference? Pain, no pain, who cares? Mosquito, no mosquito, bring it on!" I watched these thoughts and others. I thought, "Hell, they could torture me, what difference does it make? It's only my body. Yes, I'll feel feelings. Yes, I'll feel pain, but what does it matter? Is it me that will suffer? Who is me anyway? How can I suffer when there is no me? I can only suffer as long as I'm invested in a me, something that lasts, goes untainted and unchanged, and what the hell does that? Nothing. Nothing does that. There's only experience after experience, one after another in an endless succession."

I sat there grinning and breathing. The feeling stayed with me for most of the rest of the day. It didn't last. But, hey, that's the point, right? What does? And of course, neither my teacher nor anyone else ever said anything about the mosquitoes or the screen. That's why, to this day, one of my favorite quotes is Mark Twain's, "I've lived through some terrible things in my life. Some of which have actually happened!"

Basketball Stardom

I always wanted to be a basketball star, even if it meant I had to go to China to do it.

When I was a high schooler, I fantasized about being a college star. I wanted to be a giant, well-coordinated center. Though Wilt Chamberlain was my childhood hero, those were the starring days of Bill Walton at UCLA, and his quickness and court savvy astonished me. I was a willowy one hundred sixty-five pounds at six foot five when my growth stalled. I knew if I grew another six inches and put on seventy-five pounds of pure muscle, I could be a star just like him. Only in this fantasy, not only was I a star *like* him, I was a star *with* him; through perfect dream logic, when I was coming up through the college ranks (usually on my hometown team at the University of Illinois) Bill was still a star at UCLA. In every fantasy I played out in my head, we would invariably meet in the final game of the NCAA Tournament, the national championship to be decided by the titanic struggle between two of the game's all-time great centers. Yes, I was a teenage stoner.

There was an additional sociological twist. This was the late sixties, so I admired Bill for more than just his basketball skill. Long before he was a cranky TV sports analyst, he was well-known for his visibility on political and social issues, notably his anti-war activism. Certainly, there's no mistaking a celebrated six-foot-eleven ball player at campus rallies. I fancied myself a bit of a radical as well. So, in this standard-issue jock fantasy of sports stardom, there was a vivid contemporary coloring: not only were the game's greatest centers meeting head-on in the championship, they were also college basketball's most renowned hippies! Bill and I were free spirits who refused to compromise our values by having our hair cut short by military-minded coaches. We were activists who never could decide if we should stand for "The Star-Spangled Banner" before the game because that could have been interpreted as support for the Vietnam War. Instead, we began our championship game at center court with what was then called a "soul handshake."

In the final minutes with the score tied—both of us having played brilliantly, of course—we looked over at each other, and, by prearranged signal, we went on strike. We refused to go out and play. Picture Scottie Pippen's notorious refusal to play in the last eight seconds of that infamous 1994 Chicago Bulls playoff game against the New York Knicks coupled with the political meaning and impact of Tommie Smith and John Carlos' black power salute on the 1968 Olympic podium. In my fantasy, with both coaches exhorting us to "go out there and KILL!" Bill and I sat back like hirsute Buddhas and smiled. By refusing to play, Bill and I nobly rose above the "Destructiveness Fostered by the Devastating Spirit of Competition with its Source in the Capitalist Ethic." Up to that point in the game, we had played with great deference and concern for each other's safety and well-being. At that point, we stopped altogether, withholding our labor in a conscious act of protest over the exploitation of our services for questionable ends. Winning at all costs fostered Vietnam. Competition was for the unenlightened; Bill and I were beyond that. It never mattered who won the game; cooperation was the victor. Often the game was never even finished; it simply broke down in confusion, pulled apart by the impact of our peaceful protest. We created a Brechtian rupture in the television myth—Sports Competition Über Alles. Even though we loved the game dearly, we were willing to sacrifice our passion for our ideals.

While other players were off in bars drinking after the game, Bill and I would share a contemplative joint along the riverfront. To this day, when people come up and ask for our autographs, I still can't say who's the better player.

Unfortunately, when I was in junior high school, I could never make the team. Twice I suffered through the ritual humiliation of try-outs. I told myself I was surely turned down because the coaches had not even given me a good look; they predetermined who they were going to select. Perhaps. Most likely I just wasn't good enough. This contributed to my decision to switch schools after eighth grade and go to the small, semi-elite high school on campus—the one for pro-fessors' kids. That school had a tradition of losing most of its games stretching back at least ten years. I was probably the first person ever to come to Uni High for the basketball program. Of course, calling it a "basketball program" is a misnomer; there was no program. Everyone who showed up got to play. I knew I could be a star.

And I was. I was told I was the second-tallest player who ever played at the school. I guess intellectuals don't come in large sizes. (Then again, how do you explain Bill Russell, Kareem Abdul-Jabbar, David Robinson, Chris Bosh, Tim Duncan, and others?) Even though I became co-captain, leading rebounder, scorer, and MVP in my senior year, my high school career did have its downs with its ups.

Uni High provided notoriously low pay for teachers, especially in phys ed. Invariably, teachers came and went, usually staying only a year or two. For many, it was their first job after graduate school. Only the most dedicated teachers lasted years. I don't know where our coach came from during my junior year or where he went after, but he was one of those military-model coaches who found himself in an unfortunate circumstance with the proud losing tradition of our school. It didn't take long to break him in.

Before practice began that junior year in 1971, rumors were fly-ing that he was going to insist that everybody cut their hair and keep it short for the season. Sure enough, at the team's first meeting, he calmly stated that the game of basketball demanded a kempt personal appearance. The norm of the day, certainly. At that moment, I just as calmly decided I was not going to play basketball that year. In retrospect, the cold calm of that decision astounds me considering how much I loved the game, especially given that I had come to the school partly for that purpose. But in the back of my mind, I also knew there wouldn't be much of a team without me, which gave me some leverage.

During the initial games of the season, I was busy playing Donald in the school production of *You Can't Take It with You*. How I, a White person, came to play the role of the play's only Black male says a lot about my high school. None of the school's few African Americans had—quite understandably—tried out for the part. As written, the part painfully recalls Stepin Fetchit—racist to the core. Besides, most of the school's Black males were busy playing on the basketball team. As a joke, I tried out for the part and was immediately handed the role. There was no competition; no one else was foolish enough. Our drama teacher completely failed to confront the salient social issues of the drama and our performance. I went along with the flow, saying and doing nothing. In my own unconscious racism, a White guy playing a Black role only added to the hilarity. Our director/teacher hadn't addressed the issue of makeup for me and my scene partner, Rheba—another White person playing a Black role. Until opening night. Then the makeup artist looked at our director and, rightfully concerned, asked the question. The director paused. Is it possible she was only thinking about the issue for the first time? She shrugged, told her, "You decide," and walked away. We ended up going on stage in what might be called brownface.

Many White people in the audience never realized we were playing African Americans. Another sign, no doubt, of the school's overall lack of racial sensitivity. They thought we were Puerto Rican, Italian, or just well-tanned. I do remember the school's few Black kids sitting together in the front row laughing hysterically whenever we were on stage. Maybe their laughter was out of discomfort. Who knows? I didn't ask.

As the basketball season progressed without me, my hair got longer and longer, and I was growing a beard. The team was losing miserably. Our standard "moral victories" of ten- to twenty-point losses were upended by real routs of fifty, sixty, and seventy points. I was arguably the school's best player. Why I wasn't playing was an open secret. I had altogether forgotten about it, seemingly determined to devote my full expendable energies to drugs and alcohol. One day, soon after the play ended, the coach caught up with me in the hall. "Enjoyed your performance in the play," he began. It was an innocent enough opening. But here's where it needs to be said: the coach was a Black man. And of course, this changed everything. Was he kidding? Being sarcastic? I didn't detect any sarcasm, but it's hard to imagine he was serious, speaking one Black man to "another." Anyway, I was pondering these and other complexities when he said, "Think you'd be interested in playing for the team now?"

"Sure, but not if I have to cut my hair."

"OK." Then as an afterthought, "But let's keep this between you and me."

And so, it came that I rejoined the team, and it was a private arrangement between him, me, and every little farm town in East Central Illinois. I'll never forget all the laughing, hooting, and catcalls when they saw me run into the gym with a fuzzy half-beard and foot-long ponytail. There were more than a few times I wished I hadn't been so obstinate. Try concentrating on game-winning free throws with a dozen courtside rednecks boisterously pleading for a date after the game. They laughed themselves silly. Being a basketball anomaly definitely did not begin with my trip to China.

(Unattributed Photograph
Uni High Yearbook 1973)

My presence on the team provided an immediate boost and we soon returned to our standard ten- to twenty-point losses. The coach got his revenge though. In the final game of the season—the opening round of the state tournament (which we invariably lost)—he sat me on the bench the whole game. The proximal cause, as I recollect, was that I was late for the bus. Or practice. Or something. I think we both knew the real reason. When I looked questioningly at him, he simply glared at me. In the second half, I took to sitting down at the end of the bench like Dennis Rodman did years later while playing for the Chicago Bulls, stretching out and pretending to snooze, playing with towels, and trying to amuse myself. I wouldn't even join team huddles during time-outs. When he tried to embarrass me further by putting me in for the last few minutes, I simply refused. Perhaps in that moment, my teenage Bill Walton fantasy finally found its far less glorious, real-life counterpart.

Senior year was my glory. In typical Uni fashion, we had a new coach. We actually won six games, three of which were part of an unheard of three-game winning streak in the middle of the season. The local paper started putting exclamation marks in the headlines of their (still minuscule) stories: "Uni Wins Again!!!" The nominal star of our ragamuffin squad, the paper always prefaced my name with reference to my height. It was never "Fred Marx this" or "Fred Marx that." It was always "Tall, six-foot-five Fred Marx" as if "tall, six foot five" were the first two parts of an unwieldy first name. And it was never, ever "Bearded, ponytailed Fred Marx." Even if we were a liberal high school, this was still a Republican newspaper in farm country.

Whether it was his nature or he was acting on good advice, our new coach maintained a permissive attitude toward me. One exemplary event happened later in the year, illustrating our understanding of each other. The vice principal came to our PE class one morning as we were warming up to play basketball. He asked us to carry some chairs from the first floor to the fourth-floor attic. Everyone started to run off when I launched into a diatribe. "No, I'm not going to carry those chairs! For starters, there are employees of this university, *unionized* employees who are supposed to do this work, who are *paid* to do this work. If you're going to pay me what they get, that's one thing. But I'm certainly not going to carry those chairs and take away the rightful work of these union workers. I'm no scab! Secondly, this is my PE class. I'm here for physical *education*. I'm not about to give up the time set aside for education for some other purpose..." Blah, blah, blah, you get the picture. In response, from both the VP and my fellow classmates, I got one of those slack-jawed, bug-eyed looks that Hollywood likes to pass off as comedy under the rubric "reaction shot." The coach just smiled. I smiled back sheepishly and started shooting again. He knew all I really wanted was to play ball.

(Unattributed Photograph
Uni High Yearbook 1973)

Since my graduation, the school seems to have returned to its more widely recognized tradition of cranking out computer whizzes, chess prodigies, and near-winless basketball seasons. A year or two after I left, Uni went on a losing streak that lasted over four seasons. I heard about it as the streak neared one hundred losses and the school was making national news. In true non-conformist style, the team then won a game, just one short of tying the national loss record. It may have been a losing tradition, Uni High boys' basketball, but it was a jolly one.

Traveling in Europe some years later, especially while going to film festivals in Cannes and Zagreb, I often handed out business cards. Listed fourth in a five-point list of nominal skills, after "film critic, projectionist, and half-inch video production" was "freelance basketball player." (My fifth skill—"great potato salad"—got me laughs and a few invitations to potlucks.) My fantasy at that time was to land a job on some semi-professional European squad, hoping they'd accept my cheaply printed card as ample proof I could play without bothering to verify my skills on the court. There was a team in my German home-town of Freiburg that let me practice with them, but that was as far as it went. Some years later, by virtue of ribald stories from an American friend who was six foot eight and twice my bulk—a man who played semi-pro ball in Italy, Germany, and Argentina—I was finally, if wholly vicariously, able to satisfy my fantasy life of travel, money, drugs, and women courtesy of the game of basketball.

God knows it never happened in China. I should know from my high school days that when I'm one of the better players on the team we're in big trouble. And so it was with the Tianjin University teachers' team. I was not even the biggest player. We had a center who was almost my height and nearly double my weight who proved a real asset under the boards. That is, whenever you could find him there. Partly due to completely inadequate coaching, our own Shaquille O'Neal could often be found dribbling the ball outside the key. For a large man, he was amazingly deft as a ballhandler—a skill I never really acquired—and he could drive to the hoop with abandon. Though he couldn't shoot worth a damn, I did not want to be the one to suggest he should be doing something other than hoisting ridiculously long shots. No Steph Curry was he.

Years before Yao Ming, there was Mu Tiezhu, the giant eight-footer from Tibet who played on the Chinese national team. Fortunately for the teams Mu played against, he could barely run and was completely unable to jump. Every time his feet left the floor, he was taking a breathtaking risk. But it was foolish to downplay the rebounding and intimidation factor he brought. The days of the average Chinese citizen being smaller and weaker than the average Westerner have now largely ended due to the increased measure of meat and dairy in the national diet. The day the average Chinese male athlete actually matches his Western counterpart in height and strength is now here. This was not the case in 1983.

We lost one game by over forty points. I didn't want to point out to my teammates that it was nothing I wasn't used to. It was clear from the beginning that we were outmatched. We could only field a team of five, and that included the guy who was only on the team because he served as my translator. His very broken English matched my very broken Chinese nicely and we managed to confuse and distract each other on the court a lot. I played my best game, pumping hook shot after hook shot, only to run downcourt to try to fend off the flawless opposition's fast break. I seemed to be the only person on the team concerned by the fact that we were beaten on fast breaks on every play, *even after made baskets*!

The exercise was good, though, and the running helped keep me warm. We often played in outdoor arenas exposed to the winter elements. Playing indoors wouldn't have made a difference since, back then, nothing much indoors was heated anyway. Though the rare chances we got to play indoors did help cut down the occasional gusts of snow I faced heading downcourt.

Indoors or out, we always played on hard-packed dirt. The ball took some strange bounces, but I was on the lookout more for puddles and freezing mud. The fans—and there were many (even more when word got out that an American was playing)—would pack the stands sipping tea and munching on sunflower seeds. Unlike my experience with fans from opposing teams in East Central Illinois, these fans never asked me out on dates. They were far too respectful to catcall. I was used to getting stared at off the court, so it wouldn't have bothered me either way. I typically gathered a crowd of thirty or more every time I went shopping. "Hey, look! The Westerner's buying underpants!" When I invited an attractive Chinese colleague to ice cream at the downtown parlor, where only the most powerful communist cadres ate on the third and highest floor, we drew many stares. I understood only later that acting upon my sweet tooth was tantamount to a proposition of marriage. The third floor was where many Tianjin suitors brought their prospective brides to propose. It was likely the moment our voyeurs were hoping to witness. As we filed out after a game, I asked my translator what some in the crowd were saying about me. He said that my hook shot was much admired. Other comments essentially boiled down to, "But he ain't nothin' much."

Though I'm known to occasionally respect omens, I was remarkably inattentive to the portent of events after our first game: I lost both my home and away uniforms. They must have come loose from the rattrap on the back of my bike. But that wasn't the portent. When I asked the team liaison whether they could replace them for me, I was told that it didn't matter. Sure enough, in contrast to all the other teams, I noticed how with each successive game more and more of my team members were clad in shorts and T-shirts. Did they have problems with the spring tension in their bike racks too? Did they leave them in the wash? Later I learned that the uniforms were highly prized items that were probably sold on the black market. Likely, my uniforms were stolen. Nonetheless, the lack of uniform dress on the team fed my disillusionment and my growing estimation of us as a ragtag group of undisciplined players. It's too bad. I really wanted to take my uniforms back to the States as souvenirs. But who was I to complain about a dress code?

Our practice sessions consisted most memorably of one tortuous drill in which three people would race against each other to make ten shots from outside what later became known as the three-point line—all the while using the same ball and fetching our own rebounds. (How this occurred before the actual addition of the three-point shot to the game was a kind of uncanny augury.) The last person to finish ten had to start all over again with the next group. This could, and did, go on indefinitely for center types like me. The fact that this drill brutally punished those who rarely shot from further than fifteen feet away from the basket never seemed to occur to the coach. Maybe doing drills like this made Larry Bird great, but it drove me crazy. After four successive sequences where I was the last person to complete the drill, I was ready to quit the team.

The other memorable drill—presumably to develop foot agility, but probably more for fun—was to play a quick game of soccer right there on the basketball court using the basket supports as goals. Like many other drills, we did this only once. Training, like our on-court play, was not the most disciplined.

I never knew who our opponents were. Or where we were playing. Or when. My translator would simply show up at my apartment before game time and escort me by bike to the venue. When I explained that it might help to know the schedule in advance, he shrugged and basically said he didn't know either. "No one does." In those days, "public information" had little to do with the public. Still does, in fact. But it didn't matter much whether I showed up to play or not; the Chinese equivalent of "no biggie."

I had to learn the rules of the international game as I went along. In one game, I believe it was our close loss to Tianjin Tool and Die Factory #3, my translator warned me during a timeout. Apparently international rules, like the NBA's, stipulate that once the referee hands you the ball, you only have ten seconds to shoot. On the free throw line, I'm used to calming my body and meditating a while before shooting. He explained to me that if the referees were not expressing typical kindness to a foreigner, three of my last four free throw attempts would have been voided.

The next year I moved to Beijing and took a different job. If there was a teachers' team at my new university, I never heard about it and don't recall asking. I left China in 1985 and never returned. I never did fulfill my fantasies of basketball stardom. I drifted away from playing the game and ended up a filmmaker. Naturally, I developed new fantasies about Academy Awards and Hollywood success. Eight and a half years after leaving, I finally finished a long project that had taken almost half my adult life to complete. I never consciously set out to unify different themes from my life through film, but it just happened and there was no denying the result. It was called *Hoop Dreams* and it took me to the Academy Awards.

Hitchhiking Through
Europe at Eighteen

Fred Marx helps Kurt DeMoss prepare for a senior
math exam.

Unattributed photograph, Uni High Yearbook 1973

M y traveling partner Kurt DeMoss basically wore two monocles. His
glasses had deteriorated to the point that only a slight nose bridge
was left between them. The so-called temples had broken off. He
managed to hold the monocles on his face by threading pieces of

string through the lens rims, then carefully measuring them and tying them off so they'd fit around his ears. These were not the only things he owned that were falling apart.

It was common to see him sewing his clothes, backpack, or shoes whenever we made camp in the evening. When I would stare in wonder at how he managed, yet again, to repair some essential garment with what seemed like spit and paper clips, he would look up at me, smile slightly, and respire softly, emitting something between an exhale and a laugh.

That air of innocence and wonder was as tangible around Kurt as the cloud of dust around Pigpen in *Peanuts.* Everything he said and did was true even if nothing he ever said and did was believable. He looked like one of the gnomes littering the grass around George Harrison's feet on the album cover for *All Things Must Pass.*

He once disappeared in the middle of lunch for about an hour in Budapest. For Kurt, it wouldn't be exceptional, but this was at my request. I had reconnected with a local woman I met through my family four years earlier. Fifteen at the time, we became instantly infatuated but, locked as we were into family embraces, we had no privacy to explore our raging hormones. Now I was back, fed entirely by what I considered to be a torrid correspondence, which, in truth, amounted to a friendly letter exchanged every year or two. But I was more than ready to fulfill the fantasies I'd had of her since.

We'd already met Zsusza a few times prior to the fateful lunch as she graciously showed us around the city. Kurt was always in tow. So, I asked him to make himself scarce during lunch the next day. I needed some private time to determine whether she still felt the same about me. I've always been painfully shy around women I am attracted to. Typically, I need some elaborate form of premeditation to come clean with my desires. I thought fifteen minutes might do the trick, but I wasn't sure. I asked Kurt to remain at large indefinitely.

Kurt was game for anything. Maybe because our circle of friends was stoned most of the time and our personal sense of volition seemed perpetually in question, one absurd request was as valid as any other. Kurt personified this trait. He would smile slightly, respire softly, and go along with any ridiculous thing any of us suggested.

Near the end of our lunch, Kurt slid his chair out from the table and announced he had to go to the bathroom. He made his way across the large room with his usual measured gait, trailing threads from torn jeans, lightly flapping the tile floor with a loose piece of leather from the sole of his boot. That was the last we saw of him for about an hour.

After an appropriate interval to make it clear that my conversational pivot was not premeditated, I turned to reminisce with Zsusza about our meeting four years ago when the connection between us went unexplored. "Yes," she agreed. "But that was a long time ago." The finality in her voice told me all I needed to know. She also mentioned her boyfriend. At that point, my agenda was spent. The entire conversation took less than a minute.

We spent the next fifty-five minutes waiting for Kurt to return. I was more than happy to close the door on lunch and never see Zsusza again. I had nothing of importance to say. I wanted to run. I gamefully tried to make small talk. Zsusza asked repeatedly, with increasing alarm, what happened to Kurt. I shrugged and pretended I didn't know. "He's spacey." That was true. "Maybe he has diarrhea? Maybe he rushed off to American Express to cash a check?" I couldn't imagine what he might be doing. Pitching pennies? Why I never stood up and simply went to the bathroom to fetch him, I don't know. Likely it was some perverse loyalty to my plan. It was hard enough for me to come up with the whole nefarious plot. I'm preternaturally predisposed to following through on ideas even when they're demonstrated failures. I would make a good suicide bomber. Like Napoleon, I set out to cross the Russian tundra in winter. I wasn't going to abandon the campaign due to a little snow.

Fearful that he might get arrested for loitering in the men's room, eventually I went after him. Even as an eighteen-year-old straight man, I knew enough to know that hanging out in the men's room might send a certain unintended message to gay men or to those hoping to entrap them. When it became clear that he could easily have walked from the Buda side of the river to the Pest side and back again, I left for the bathroom.

It was a large, Soviet-era tile lavatory. Dripping water echoed across the cavern. Kurt was lucky there was no attendant sitting outside collecting coins. "What have you been doing?" I laughed. I vaguely remember an answer having to do with counting tiles. I was sorry and ashamed that he hadn't had the sense to walk out of the restaurant and at least explore the neighborhood. I don't recall arriving at some suitable story for him to tell. But we must have.

Back at the table, Zsusza shrieked, "What happened to you?!" No doubt Kurt laughed sheepishly before launching into some outlandish story. Or maybe he said he fixed the broken sole of his shoe and lost track of time sewing.

Whatever he said, I'm sure Zsusza thought it ridiculous. But this being Kurt, I'm confident it also sounded like the truth. Maybe she lobbed us both into the mental framework of her own Cold War understanding, concluding that Westerners are as crazy as communist propaganda had taught her.

Zsusza and I never wrote to each other again.

This should have been a lifelong lesson for me. Unfortunately, I'm a slow learner. Like most teens, I carried the flame of an almost relationship far beyond the realms of reason. Once a moment passes, it will never return. Unlike most teens, I didn't get that memo until late in my twenties, having just repeated the same mistake, this time pursuing a flame ignited in a 1978 attraction to a Serbian woman by inviting her to visit me in China in 1983. By the time Sonja arrived from Belgrade in 1984, I had been with my new Finnish girlfriend for six months. At this point, Heli had the good sense to break up with me, leaving me with my Serbian friend who had become a follower of Satan.

Back in 1978, a week or so after the Zsusza debacle, Kurt and I were hitchhiking down the Turkish-Aegean coast. Turkey and Greece were on the brink of war over the island of Cyprus. A truck driver dropped us in the middle of nowhere in the middle of the night. No lights, no gas station, nothing. There wasn't even moonlight. I barely remember seeing the intersection in the road. We wearily trudged into a wooded hillside in search of flat ground to pitch our sleeping bags.

I've always been a light sleeper. But I was on the verge of sleep when I heard a slight rustling in the woods. "Kurt! You hear that?" Already unconscious, Kurt moaned "Hmmm..." and didn't move. The rustling got louder. A bear? Snakes? I knew nothing about wildlife in Western Turkey or, in fact, anything about Western Turkey. I was on high alert but too afraid to turn on my flashlight. Propping my head up, I willed myself to see into the black. I thought I saw multiple shadowy figures moving toward us. Suddenly, I could make out guns.

I jumped out of my sleeping bag and threw my hands up. "*Studenti! Touristi! Americanski!*" Not only did I not know a single word of Turkish, I couldn't even imitate a Turkish accent. What poured out of my mouth was Russian pidgin. Instantly, multiple spotlights flashed on. A squad of eight to ten soldiers in full battle dress holding machine guns surrounded us. "*Studenti! Touristi! Americanski!*" I was an idiot on autopilot. Terror will do that to you. Kurt stood too. Fortunately, we were both still dressed. For once, Kurt's clothes stayed on his body.

"Pass! Passport!" They barked at us. We whipped them out. Orders in Turkish to the subordinates ensued. While they searched our bags, they scrutinized our passports, flashing their lights from them to our faces and back again. There was discussion among them. It couldn't have been pleasant to rifle through dirty socks, dog-eared maps, and half-eaten clumps of feta. Clearly, they had no clue what to make of us.

They motioned for us to grab our stuff. They led us down the hill back to the road, shining their lights into the trees on the other side, making it clear that's where we should throw our sleeping bags. Presumably reassured that we were not Greek invaders on an undercover mission, they disappeared.

It still amazes me that they didn't take us somewhere for questioning. Maybe our expressions of unadulterated fear worked in our defense. Why they didn't shoot first and ask questions later, I'll never know. But I'm grateful. Someone even had the courtesy to explain in broken English that we had bedded down on a coastal hillside crawling with big guns ready to open fire on Greek invaders. Thank god for professional soldiers.

It took some hours for my heart to stop racing. Eventually, I fell asleep because I remember waking up in the pre-dawn light and looking around. There, not one hundred yards away, was a large military camp. How we completely missed an entire company of soldiers the night before mystifies me. But I'll never question the skills of the Turkish military to maneuver in darkness under cover of absolute silence.

The next day we made it to Bodrum and enjoyed drinking coffee and watching the elders play the tile game okey. None of the ferries to Greece were running. Finally, an enterprising Turkish sailboat owner decided to make a run for it, charging eight foreign tourists fifty dollars each for the fourteen-mile ride through open water to Kos. Once out of the harbor, he reeled in the Turkish flag and rang up the Greek. The Greek harbor police were not amused but allowed us to disembark before chasing the ferryman the hell out of there. I'll never forget the image of Kurt sitting on the prow of the sailboat, looking back at us with a tranquil smile, one leg sprawled on the gunwale, his fraying shorts torn up the middle, completely oblivious to his exposed testicles basking in the sun.

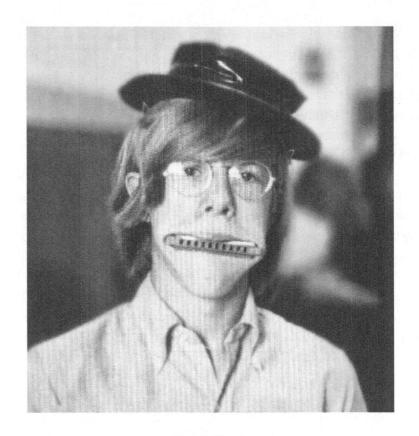

Kurt DeMoss
November 12, 1955 – October 1, 1979
(Unattributed Photograph
Uni High Yearbook 1972)

Meditation Hijinks

I proudly call myself a drama queen. If you're a filmmaker and don't love drama, then something is wrong. If sufficient drama doesn't arrive for you through the course of standard everyday events, then you might unconsciously create it. Watch out.

On a three-week silent meditation retreat, I once got so hungry for drama I picked a fight with my *dharma* teacher. I was having an elaborate romance with a fellow yogi—a lovely woman from Belgium who wore an attractive ankle bracelet and liked going barefoot. Since she and I weren't allowed to talk, exchange notes, rendezvous clandestinely in the woods for passionate romance—in fact, interact in any way, even meet each other's gazes and look into each other's eyes—I developed a fetish for those feet. The erotic highlight of my day was perusing her feet in the cloakroom where we removed our jackets and shoes. She and I were great lovers. Our relationship was intimate, authentic, and caring, albeit overly erotic. Unfortunately, it existed solely in my head. I didn't even know her name. "Vipassana Romance," we call it.

I confessed none of this to my teacher during our occasional one-on-one sessions. I didn't have to. All I had to do was relate my concern that she had missed lunch. I told him I intended to bring food to her room. He emphatically urged me not to.

"How do you know she missed lunch?"

"She never came to the dining room!"

"How do you know she's hungry?"

"She missed lunch!"

"Maybe she chose to miss lunch. Maybe she's not even hungry."

"Impossible! Who misses lunch?! She's probably starving!"

Talk about projection. I can count on one hand the times I've missed lunch in my life.

I tried to defend my indefensible actions by ratting out others, hiding one transgression by committing another. I started spilling the beans about the other subterranean romances I observed. Men holding the cafeteria door open for particular women. One young man seeking the most proximate location possible without actually standing next to her to "join" a woman during her solo walking meditation, following her every move with his eyes. One woman directly violating protocol, saying "hello" to a male yogi in the tea room after hours. Another woman spontaneously helping a guy with his afternoon chores cleaning the dining room. Drama. Or at least what passes for it on a meditation retreat.

Those last two happened to me. The offer to assist with chores came from none other than my Belgian lover. The cauldron of hormones raging through my body heated exponentially. When I saw her duplicating my work routine by stacking chairs onto tables, I bowed ostentatiously in her direction. "What if this escalates to sweeping and mopping?" My fantasies ran wild. "Maybe we'll hose down the rubber kitchen mats!" Bowing was the one mode of recognition permitted to us. She bowed back. Oh! How many times I replayed that in my mind! She loved me! She truly loved me!

Apparently, I myself was the object of some Vipassana Romances. I wanted nothing more than to grab a cup of tea and have an intimate conversation while gazing longingly into her eyes. I wanted to bridge our unbridgeable gap, to soak in the warm bath of mutual affection. Who am I kidding? I wanted to grab her hand, sprint into the woods, and make mad, passionate love on a warm hard rock.

But I'm a rule follower. (Paradoxical, I know, since I'm also a rebel.) I couldn't bring myself to engage her. I wouldn't even look at her. The frontiers of desire get murky in *The Land of Silence and Meditation*. Sadly, deplorably, I was more committed to the path of awakening, to enlightenment, than I was to meeting the love of my life, or at least having a potentially exciting conversation. Perhaps it was an admirable choice. But at that moment, it was a terribly painful one. All I could summon was a lonely bow.

My teacher just shook his head at me. He seemed at a loss to know how to skillfully combat my multiple and varied delusions. In fact, he seemed to be getting angry. I, however, was happily, if unconsciously, fulfilling yet another delusion. Though I may not play the white knight and bring my Belgian princess chicken soup for the soul, I created drama! Something interesting was occurring: human conflict! I'm actually making a Buddhist teacher angry! I was no longer drifting at sea without a compass. I could latch on to something. Fixate. Now playing: *A Fight with my Teacher!* "Delusions of the mind are inexhaustible," said the Buddha. I volunteer to be the poster boy.

Most dramas one encounters on meditation retreats are wholesale fabrications of the mind. The whole purpose of a retreat is to create a uniform ground of experience where everything is structured and homogeneous. By providing a neutral ground of extreme regularity, retreats are designed to become a mirror to the contorted workings of your own mind. If you sit in silence long enough, whatever deep unresolved emotional issues you have, whatever unconscious drives and behavioral tics remain, will come to the fore. In that sense, your suffering will be very real. The grief, the anger, the lust, the fear, the desire... all of it will bubble to the surface. Hopefully, eventually, we learn that each wounded thought represents a choice. Do I want to engage this now? We always have that choice, whether faced with mental chimeras like Vipassana Romance, with actual memories of real horror and abuse or spinning out with fear about something that might happen. Inexhaustible means inexhaustible. If and when we choose to, meditation sessions can become the threshing floor for examining and dissolving both delusions and real traumas.

Following the "dropping in" phase of a meditation retreat—three to five days, on average—a very curious thing happens. The abnormality of the situation fades away and the daily patterns of retreat life become the new normal. People's habits and impulses from the outside world start to reappear, no matter how inappropriate in the new context. Food is one of the great bellwethers. In the early days when people are visibly mindful and more self-conscious of their behavior, walking slowly to get to lunch is the norm. It's like a footrace in reverse. Who can be the slowest to reach the feeding trough? Like the tortoise and the hare, only now the hare has abandoned the playing field and taken sole refuge in the mind. "I'm not so uncouth and unmindful as you. I'm in no hurry!" My favorite version of this story has Bugs Bunny playing the lead.

After three or four days, people suddenly speed up. They do whatever they can to get there fast. Pretense be damned! Caution is thrown to the wind. "FOOD!!!" Once in the dining room, yogis who previously have eaten slowly or eaten only modest portions heap on multiple servings and stuff the piehole with abandon.

During walking meditation, some people start humming or singing. One yogi in the meditation hall hissed "SHUSH!" to another who suffered from a seemingly unconscious tendency to snort. People going completely unconscious on a retreat designed to raise awareness—it's hilarious. All those everyday habits of personality and behavior surge back to the surface. Inexhaustible delusions of the mind ...

The peculiar sociology of community on a meditation retreat is without peer. I've always wanted to film one for a documentary. How do teachers quell all the romances blooming in the heads of deluded yogis? What do they do when someone goes so unconscious as to start dancing and singing in public? I know the answer to that one. They asked him to leave. How do they deal with insomniacs? I wish I knew because one scared the shit out of me.

In the middle of the night as I was sleepily returning from the bathroom, one guy stepped out of the spectral darkness and stared at me with terrifying intensity like I was going to leap over the second-floor balcony to swoop down on him and suck his neck dry of blood.

Freaked me out. If I could have I would have locked my door. Maybe that's why the doors don't have locks. What about people who sleep all day and won't leave their room? It happens. Depression can be as common on retreat as in everyday life.

I used to enjoy getting to the first unofficial sit at 5:30 a.m. I like the extreme quiet in the morning when only a few haunted yogis are present. I enjoy seeing the light change from darkness to dawn. Similarly, I love doing the final late-night sit after the official program ends at 9:00 p.m. The room is dark once again and deliciously quiet. For this behavior, I got Yogi Gold Stars.

One of my teachers complimented me. She thought it was healthy and wholesome. "Somebody noticed me!" I thought as I snatched my little ego morsel and retreated back to the hutch of my mind. But the truth was deeper. "Are you kidding me? What else is there to do?! You won't let us read or write. We can't talk to anyone. We can't phone home or get on the computer. No cell phones, journals, writing tools, laptops, iPads, no music of any kind, including instruments, no reading material… We can't get in the car, go out and grab a burger, or see a movie. What the hell am I supposed to do? Sit on my bed and stare at the ceiling? Except for taking long walks in the woods, from 5:30 a.m. to 10 p.m. there's literally nothing else to do." Might as well trudge to the meditation hall and meditate.

One scene I've long envisioned for a fictional rom-com script revolves around a typical midtwenties heterosexual couple. The man is on a long-term retreat. His girlfriend at home discovers a transgression—an affair, some infidelity, or some major lie he's told. She decides she won't wait. She drives to the retreat center. In the meditation hall, sixty yogis sit supreme, statue-like and silent, all eyes closed. Perfect Buddhas. A distant birdcall is the loudest sound audible through open windows. The woman takes off her shoes and glides across the room to stand in front of her lover. Aware someone is nearby, our yogi holds the pose, not peeking, the master of equipoise. She hesitates, holding her breath. Then, **CRACK**! She smacks him right across the face as hard as she can with her open hand.

Shock ripples through the room along with the echoes. Though some try not to move or peek, most bodies turn and watch, some through half-open eyes pretending to be closed. More stunned than hurt, the yogi looks up at her. "What the ... ?!" Fixing him with eyes of furor, she vehemently shushes him with a finger to her mouth. Then as quickly, silently, and effortlessly as she came, she departs, ever so softly closing the door behind her. The final shot is a wide POV of the room—some staring open-mouthed, no one moving. The door latches closed with a gentle click, the scene's final sound.

Other fictional scenes I've written in my head—yes, while supposedly meditating—naturally include hot sex where two Vipassana Romancers get it on in the dining room in the middle of the night. Or out on some remote trail in the neighboring woods where they run into each other by accident. Of course, there are dozens more variations, many involving clandestine nighttime room visits. The walls are thin and close, so maintaining silence is both the greatest challenge and the supreme delight.

Meditation retreats are rife with the possibility for humor and hijinks. Taking my experience as a starting point, I can imagine a teacher being drawn into a shouting match with an obstinate and drama-hungry yogi. I can imagine yogis dropping little notes on each other's meditation cushions, leaving them under their *zafus* and *zabutons*. You can never forget the fear factor. Anyone could rat you out and you might be kicked out at any time. Mirth and drama, inexhaustible...

I remember how outraged I was when one of my teachers asked me if I could move my *zabuton* and cushions elsewhere in the meditation hall. One of my homies in the meditation hood had complained about me. Maybe I was crying too much since I was going through the final stage of grief over a recent breakup. It's hard to cry silently, but it can be done if you let the tears fall as they may while opening your mouth as wide as possible to minimize gulps of air. Maybe all that snot was giving me trouble breathing and I was honking my nose-horn too much.

I assume it was a she since there were largely only women nearby. Maybe the other scenes parading across the TV channels of my mind were making me chuckle too often and too loudly. Maybe my socks smelled bad. Maybe she didn't like that I sat on two *zafus* instead of one. I don't recall the reason my teacher gave me, but I do remember feeling outraged. The pettiness! I thought we were supposed to learn to accept and accommodate everything! "The Other is not the problem. Your unwillingness to accept them is the problem." It's laughingly similar to problems homeowners have with neighbors. With your *zabuton* mat and cushions, you can't exactly build a ten-foot wall between properties and sic your dog on their cat.

People do approach those spaces like their homes. Or their beds. Or their cribs. Favorite blankets, favorite cushions, changes of socks... I'm surprised I never saw teddy bears. If water could be brought in, there'd be water bottles everywhere. Or vases of flowers. As for me, I had a glucometer for testing my blood sugar tucked discreetly under my *zabuton*. If needed, it was there for testing before, after, or, in real emergencies, *during* meditation sessions. I also had glucose, my glasses, Kleenex, and don't tell, a pen that I used to first plant the seeds of this chapter.

Nobody is Accountable

Ghosting has always been one of my pet peeves. Long before internet dating perfected the art, I was ticked off by ghosters. People who say, "I'll call you next week"; "I'll get that letter to you tomorrow"; "I'll circle back with you soon"; "We'll be there Friday to follow up"; "You'll have it by the end of the day," and then … nothing. No phone calls, no emails, no more responses to anything. Sometimes they go underground for a certain period of time and reemerge. Typically, they disappear forever. No word. No goodbye. No, "Sorry, I'm out of here." Nothing. A black hole. I actually would prefer it if people said, "I never want to see you again. Goodbye and good riddance!" "Don't call. Don't write … Drop dead, fuckface!" "Get out of my life, you loser!" "Make like a politician caught in a scandal and disappear." "Do what billionaires do to avoid taxes—go to the Cayman Islands!"

Sometimes there's foreshadowing. They'll hint that they're planning to ghost you. They'll resist your every invitation to set a time for a future meeting by being vague. "Talk soon!" What they're really saying is, "Don't call me. I'll call you. Or, maybe I won't." I've learned to ask people, "When will be a good time to circle back with you if I don't hear from you first?" That catches people off guard. Then they'll have to commit. The smart ones, quick on their feet, won't do it. They'll stay vague and, of course, commit to contacting me first. But if they do answer my question, all they're committing to is allowing me to bug them again, which is just one more invitation for them to ghost me. "That guy? Again?!" Nonetheless, I dutifully put a tickler in my calendar and follow up, praying for a different result. Typically, I'm ghosted again. My least favorite ghosting, one that I actually learned in Hollywood where it was made famous, is "let's do lunch." What they're really saying is, "I'm happy to have lunch together. Twenty-five years from now, I'll have a picnic on your grave."

At this point in my life, the number of people who've ghosted me must be around a thousand. Family, friends, business partners, board members, film crew, call centers, clerks, mechanics, donors, doctors, lawyers, plumbers, and painters... People who've promised me money, support, service, information, feedback, advice, their car, their foxy sister... it might as well have been the moon. Does integrity really mean so little nowadays? How do people do that and live with themselves? Is this a byproduct of the "be nice" generation where it's "too hurtful" to tell someone you can't and won't keep a simple agreement? If you're someone like that, brace yourself, I'm going to be hurtful. Fuck you!

Typically, it's a function of privilege. The more money and power someone has, the more entitled they feel to ignore any agreement they made with you. For them, there are no repercussions. Who's going to get in their face and say, "Hey, fuckface. What about that $10,000 donation you promised me?" Power and privilege inure them. No one wants to risk receiving future crumbs from their table.

I recognize the internal dynamics that keep people from responding. Usually, it's shame. People feel ashamed when they haven't done what they promised, so it's easier to disappear. Reach for the invisibility cloak! Picture tens of thousands of people ducking under their desks every day. Some people live their whole lives down there wishing they couldn't be seen and hoping that people will just go away. What are you, three years old?! There are hundreds of kids walking around like that right now laughing their heads off. "No one can see me if my head is in this paper bag!"

Once someone is moving down that shame spiral, getting them to reverse course is almost impossible. Almost anything you say or do is going to make things worse. You can try to be direct: "You said you were going to put me in touch with that donor." You can try to be gentle and indirect: "Really sorry I missed your call. Can we reschedule?" You can try to hold them accountable: "I was waiting by the phone at 1:00 p.m. when you said you'd call." None work. Any approach will just make them defensive. If they're really stuck in shame, they'll simply project their self-loathing onto you for making them feel bad. "Fuck him! Who does he think he is? I've got more important things to do than tend to *his* wants." Quicker than you can say, "get out of my life," they'll be writing *you* off forever for something *they* haven't done.

I once asked my Board President Michael Bonahan for advice on how to deal with ghosters. This is the letter he suggested sending them:

> *Dear Ghost,*
>
> *I've been expecting to hear back from you since we _____ . I was looking forward to receiving _____ from you. Did I mis-understand your offer/commitment? I've inventoried my own actions since our last meeting and I can't find anything that would place me out of integrity with you. If there is something I'm missing, please let me know.*
>
> *If not, I ask that you take the time to check in with yourself and see if you are still willing to work with me in the challenge to better our world for youth, families, and communities. If your answer is "no," then please do me the courtesy of responding to save us both time.*
>
> *With all best wishes,*
> *Frederick*

It's a wonderful model. If only it worked. I've sent it to at least five people and still haven't heard back from them. What I really want to do is shout a hearty "fuck you!" at them and leave a nasty message on their voice mail or email. Tell them they let me down and they won't have me to kick around anymore (à la Richard Nixon after he lost the California gubernatorial election in 1962). "I spent six months, four phone calls, and seven emails trying to track you down and nix, nada, nothing. Thanks for wasting my time, asshole!" My shadow truth? I do enjoy burning bridges. But I try my best not to. Instead, I fantasize about getting revenge on them by giving them backhanded public compliments that are only marginally more subtle. Thanking them, in absentia, at the event they abandoned, by saying, "If it weren't for [ghoster], I never would've come to understand the true meaning of integrity." "If it weren't for [ghoster], I never would've met [my real supporter], who made this event happen." "[Ghoster] strengthened my capacity for empathy. Now I'm rededicated to finding empathy in my heart even for people I never want to see again."

It's a busy world and everyone is overwhelmed. I get it. You have to be persistent. These days, multiple contact attempts are almost required to achieve results. Persistence is a top-ten character attribute. It can actually be prized by recipients, too; those who are spinning frantically, those for whom repeated introductions or repeated reminders are necessary to break through their wall of activity and noise—especially if they're big shots. You have to hound the person, or their "people," before they even consider responding. For months, I tried to reach a famous Los Angeles doctor known for advocating mindfulness practice and emotional intelligence for teens. I spoke with his appointment secretary numerous times, but we were unable to coordinate calendars. One day, after trying one more time, she wrote back and basically said that she was done with me and would no longer respond to my requests. "Why?" I asked. "Because I don't like you," was basically her reply. Wow. That was a shock. People in the service professions, perhaps especially if they're underpaid, do it because they can. If you know some way to reach this celebrated university doctor directly, let me know. I'd love to let him know what his mindfulness staff is up to.

But that's about the rich and powerful. Mostly I'm talking about people who aren't big shots but who've already committed something to you. People who aren't in the "I'll have my people call your people" category. Call me old-fashioned, but I feel like it's not only ineffective to reach out to people multiple times to remind them of their commitment, it eventually becomes rude, however delicately you word your "friendly reminder." If they're stuck in a shame spiral and hate you for making them hate themselves, nothing will get them to respond.

There's the "now is better than later" argument, allowing you to learn who is unreliable while still early in the relationship. It's good to know when to cut your losses so you don't waste more valuable time. That is helpful. I deeply prize respondents who give me a simple "no" when I make requests. But I've had people ghost me after years of working together. I'm preternaturally committed to ethics and ethical behavior. I actually believe the world can and should function where people walk their talk, where their word is their bond. Stop and imagine what a wonderful world that would be! Where everyone keeps their agreements and follows through on what they say. Where integrity and accountability are paramount, no one lies, cheats, or steals. Politicians, corporate leaders, bureaucrats, and lawyers telling the truth and following through! We'd have paradise on Earth!

As a model for my own behavior, it does not present a problem, which is not to say that I'm perfect. I don't follow through on commitments every now and then, forgetting or overlooking them. But I'm always willing to be accountable for them. My problem is I expect other people to act in similarly honorable ways. A completely losing proposition. So, I repeatedly agonize over people's unwillingness to be accountable. I have a razor-sharp critical mind and I'll judge them sharply. I take it too far. It's become a form of religion. I quickly lose respect for them when they don't live up to my standards and damn them to hell.

Since Zen teaches us that reality is the only thing that matters, watching what human beings do, not what they say, is what matters most. Holding human beings up to any expectation of standards and beliefs about how they should behave is a surefire way to make yourself miserable. I am exhibit A. Everyone has their favorite form of self-created misery. Ghosting is mine. Having run this particular loop of suffering for most of my life, I believe I'm finally getting the lesson. I've spent far too much time engaged in this imprudent pursuit. "People should behave in honorable ways" is itself a dogma foolhardy in the extreme. I want off this karmic merry-go-round.

I forget it's not about them. It's about me. What part of me insists on holding on to any expectation they might have created? Most people aren't interested in being accountable or keeping their word. They say stuff, knowing full well they'll never follow through. It's an aspiration, something they *hope* will come to pass. Like when they say "try." "I'll try to be there." As soon as you hear that word, you should understand they'll never show up. Saying "try" is like promising to repay someone a debt by buying lottery tickets. Not only will it never happen, they've just guaranteed you it will never happen by giving themselves an out in the very words they've used to express their commitment. A red flag should not just go up, it should explode around your head like millennial fireworks. It's just wind fluttering past your ears, sounds that someone formed with their lips and exhaled with a vocalization that made them feel momentarily good. They might well have said "Gadzooks" or "Kerplonken" or "Fizzyfiddle" or "Pffffffffffft." It carries no more meaning than the sound of a plane crossing the sky or a distant dog bark.

"Flush and move on," my Zen teacher said. Those are now my watchwords. When someone makes a commitment to me, I might follow up with one or two of those "friendly reminders," but I won't take long before writing them off. Flush and move on. It might mean spending more time on the toilet, but it also means walking away without a sick stomach.

The Ten-Minute Dating Rule

[This chapter is addressed primarily to heterosexual men. If you're a woman or a gay man, some of this may or may not apply to you.]

When dating, you enter a world where everything is uncertain. You're replacing the known world with the unknown. Everything you thought you knew no longer applies. Words, looks, touches, even smells and sounds suddenly become unhinged from the semiotic systems where they formerly resided. With each new person, you land on a new planet. Gravity has shifted. On some, you practically float, weightless and free, unmoored from any system of known meaning— Crazyland. On others, you can barely lift your feet to walk, crushed by others' expectations. Some planets fall away from you just as you're about to stand and take your first step, then recede with differing speeds into the blackness of space. Ghosting.

Arguably, this is not a wise path to take for a man whose heart was recently split open after thirteen years of marriage by the death of his beloved wife, Tracy.

But date I must and date I did. I did it like I was approaching a reasonably grim job. It was something I recognized I needed to do, like flossing or exercising. Call it emotional hygiene. Though its immediate impact is somewhat the opposite, the long-term aim is to keep the mind and body healthy and whole, the masculine humming in good relationship with the feminine. Sex, love, intimacy…a well-rounded heterosexual man requires them.

Where to begin? First, there's a nearly infinite number of dating sites. Interested in interracial dating? There's a site for you. Gluten-Free Singles? Yep. Want to date a golfer or a clown? Uh-huh.

Someone who likes mullets or wears diapers? Oh, yeah! Interested only in Jewish women who like sports? I haven't found that one yet, but I'm sure it won't be long.

After my wife died was the fourth key time in my life that dating became a kind of coming out party. Back in the eighties, during test launch number one, I took a scary step and posted ads in the newspaper personals section. In more recent excursions over the last twenty years, I set up online profiles on dating sites. I did it primarily as a way to serve notice to myself that I was back in the game, willing and ready to put myself on the line to find a good woman.

Oddly, I didn't much care if I found one or not. I was happy to announce to myself and the world that I was done grieving the end of my last relationship. It was an important symbolic threshold to cross. I was open for business, ready to love and be loved again. The first two experiences never led anywhere. The third one led to my wife. The fourth one never led anywhere either; I met my beloved girlfriend Maggie without online assistance. But I never regretted any iteration of self-advertising. Dealing with the weirdness, the uncertainty, and the rejection all helped me grow as a man.

I met some wild and wacky women along the way. I was about halfway through one date when my companion literally ran away from me. All I could make out as she was running down the street was, "Oh, there's my bus! Gotta go, now. Bye!" I knew things weren't going well. I think I was done in her eyes after I tried to get her to split the dinner bill. After I got over the shock of her running after the bus, I laughed so hard I almost fell down on the sidewalk. Maybe she was afraid I would run after her and plead for us to stay together. "No! Please! Give me another chance! I can change! I'll reimburse you!"

I used to schedule blind dates for a whole evening with women I hadn't met. Experiences like the one with the rapid transit lover quickly showed me how stupid that was. So I scaled back. I would meet women only for coffee or a quick meal.

Until one day. That day I sat through a lunchtime odyssey with a woman from Neptune. In the first ten seconds of meeting her, I knew I was not only not interested in her, but I hoped I'd never see her again for as long as I lived. I couldn't bear the thought of eating food, so I didn't order. And yet I sat through forty-four agonizing minutes watching her eat her meal. If the smile that was frozen on my face had fallen off, it would've cracked the table in two.

That's when I finally got sensible. I made hard and fast rules: No, I won't exchange emails with you other than to exchange phone numbers and work out logistics for getting together. No, I won't talk with you on the telephone beyond our one first call and some brief preliminaries getting to know you. And when we finally get together? Ten minutes max. That's it. No kidding. I won't even order a cup of tea in case it takes too long to cool and drink. I do take a glass of water. It can come in handy marching through the hot sands of desperation.

Why no phoning or emailing, but just a brief, initial face-to-face? Because I learned. Lots of women are going to sound fantastic on the telephone. Sexy, sultry voices wagging long, shapely fingers at you, hinting at big invitations: "Come on over, big fella." Then when you meet you realize, "Yep, she's got a great voice. Unfortunately, that's it. A great voice and nada." Lots of women are going to be clever and funny and flirty on email. But the bulk of your relationship will not consist of phone calls and emails. (If it does, well, you need more advice than I can give you.) Nothing is as important as someone's human presence. What they look, feel, and act like. How they move. How they look at you. What is it you see when you look into their eyes? How do they react when a dog suddenly barks? How do they blow their nose? How do they smell? What do they do when they suddenly spill coffee on their starched white blouse? How good is their dentist? Those are the things that matter. And in ten minutes or less, you can answer the only question that really matters: Do I want to see her again? Nine out of ten times, the answer will be no.

I tried this out on Tinder. I matched with a number of women. Most never responded at all, even after I sent a hello text. Were they just baiting the hook to see if they got any bites? A few responded with a flirty line or two, saying nothing of substance. But every single one disappeared when I dropped the hammer:

> Please forgive me if this sounds crass or crude, but I'd like to meet for ten minutes somewhere for tea. In my experience, I can learn more about someone who I might be compatible with in a brief face-to-face visit than in hours of phone conversations, texts, or emails. Following that first visit, we're then both free to choose each other for a subsequent, longer visit at another time or not. Let me know if that sounds amenable to you.

Not a single woman deigned this statement worthy of a response.

Many women talk in their bios about not seeking hookups but wanting to meet sincere, well-intentioned men. Does the statement above not qualify? To me, ghosting is just plain rude, as if to say, "I posted a profile here just to see if anyone responds. I'm really not interested in meeting anyone. I just want to see how well my profile's working." Is this the underlying reality? I must be terribly old-fashioned to believe that every human being deserves the dignity of a response, even if that response is "I'm leaving now. Have a nice life."

Did I lose the opportunity to meet plenty of women this way? Probably. I don't care. Life is too short to repeat this particular ring of hell. Think of all the time you've saved, the agony avoided. And that one in ten? If you call her the next day, and the next, and the next, and she never returns your calls because she doesn't want to see *you* again, well, again, think of all the time you've saved.

The ten-minute dating rule didn't stop me from meeting my wife. Months after I had given up on dating, months after I had forgotten I still had a profile on a website, she contacted me. That first ten-minute meeting turned out to be five because we couldn't find each other at the café. I made damn sure I had an unbreakable appointment afterward. Did she think I was a bit crazy? Maybe. But on our single preliminary phone call, I explained to her why I had that rule. And she got it. Her time was precious too. For years afterward, she laughed hysterically every time she recounted how our first meeting barely happened due to my ten-minute dating commandment.

Why bother at all, you might ask. I get it. I understand people who choose celibacy because they can't stand the humiliations of dating. But for me, François Truffaut's 1977 movie title—*The Man Who Loved Women*— says it all. I love their beauty and allure. I love their minds and the way they smell. I love being intimate with them, talking softly, only inches from their face, and feeling their breath while gazing into their eyes. No doubt all that only qualifies me for typical heterosexual male status. I certainly love the shapely female form, and perhaps even worship female beauty. But it's the mind that captures me the most. A brilliant mind is a woman's most erotic instrument. Dating taught me a new word for this—sapiosexual. As long as you can think originally, capable of reaching for and finding new ideas or expressing old ideas in new and original ways, the flame will never die.

But that's assuming you get started. Just getting to the point where you can meet a woman is a challenge. That's getting to first base. That's success. Not kissing. Kissing is like a home run in the dating game. It takes a lot of work just to get eyeball to eyeball. First, you have to get to the ballpark and into uniform; that's setting up your online dating profile. Then you've got to be put in the lineup; that's attracting her attention and getting on her radar. Then, like a pinch hitter, you may have only one chance at bat. What you say in that first text or email may be your last chance. This only reinforces the logic of the ten-minute dating rule for me. If you're going to be ghosted at any moment, why not have it happen after you've at least met face-to-face?

But if all goes well on that first meeting, the challenges only increase. It's all too easy to spin into a mind-stream "How much does she like me? Will she find my beard scratchy? Is my breath OK? Am I too tall or hunched over? What if she doesn't like my sense of humor?" What am I, twelve?! This is embarrassingly juvenile behavior for a man past middle age. Mostly, the obsessions have to do with sex. After my wife died, I hadn't had it in so long—and it was even longer since I had *good* sex—that the prospect filled me with volcanic excitement and energy, which isn't an outlook that readily neutralizes mind waves. If I didn't strictly limit my online dating time to ten minutes in the morning and ten in the evening, I knew my soul was already in the possession of the dating devil.

Half the world seems to be online seeking a relationship with someone else. The vast numbers seem to compound the problem of finding someone. It turns human beings into readily disposable commodities. Why bother investing real energy and attention in getting to know someone? Swipe left. There's always another. Who is truly appreciative of any one person or encounter? Swipe left. If the guy you're with happens to be wearing a sock with a hole in it, swipe left. I got matched online with a beautiful woman. According to the website algorithm, we were ninety-seven percent compatible. Ninety-seven percent! I actually tend to trust that algorithm because it's based on hundreds of questions—some are ridiculous, most are reasonably thoughtful, and a few are even demanding. I reached out and received this reply, "Oh, I remember you. Your profile said you need sex only once or twice a week. I need it every day. Goodbye!"

It's true that sex is a bottom-line standard for most people, a more weighted and fraught variable than most. If the sex stars are not one hundred percent in alignment, it's typically a deal-breaker. But I didn't say I was averse to sex every day; I just don't *need* it every day. Isn't that a rather trivial reason to decide not to meet someone you're supposedly ninety-seven percent compatible with? How superficial can you be?

To judge your compatibility with a complex human being based on one lone variable out of a thousand strikes me as self-defeating, especially over time. Once you get into a relationship and begin to discover your many differences, will you let one difference sink the ship? Don't most people by their late twenties understand that a perfect mate doesn't exist? Any lover you take on is going to become problematic in ways you've never foreseen, no matter how compatible you both are initially.

Online dating feeds addiction no less than online porn. Are there studies yet that prove it? If not, let me be the first to warn you. Online dating is crack. It is a never-ending invitation to fantasy. It's easy to spend hours lost in reverie. Perhaps this is the adult equivalent of teens addicted to video games. Since I have little idea how women experience this process—other than as a cauldron of fear and uncertainty tossed into a roiling sea of horny men—let me address my remaining comments to my male brothers, you libidinous bastards!

Online dating means looking at pictures of beautiful women and reading wonderful things about them. The unspoken, unacknowledged invitation is not so much to reach out and contact them but to enter dreamland and fantasize about how wonderful the two of you will be together. Should you reach out and be lucky enough to receive a response, the projections deepen—"Now she really wants me. We're off to paradise…" Pretty soon, you'll be constructing elaborate mental castles of your future together before you've even met. Then if you meet and have the fortune (misfortune?) of being attracted to her, god help you. You will walk away with that volcano of sexual energy pumping hot molten thoughts into your exploded brain.

Is this conducive to the mindful formation of relationships? No. It's conducive to your body releasing volumes of dopamine to Roto-Root your system with ecstatic energy. I wonder how much dating companies are aware of this. I wonder how much, like the tobacco companies, they calculate what dosage of the drug (fantasy) they need to deliver to the consumers (lonely people) within each unit of measure (a single person's profile) to keep them coming back for more (addiction). Dating sites do have an advantage over tobacco or alcohol—you can't die from an overdose. Are there twelve-step groups like Daters Anonymous? Perhaps not yet. But the pipelines of people seeking recovery from dating sites must flow directly into other twelve-step groups like Sex and Love Addicts Anonymous. Hopefully, compulsive online daters will find the help they need there. I took heart in limiting morning online dating to my time on the crapper.

How did I deal with all these vagaries, uncertainties, and over-whelming energies? By remaining honest and real. That's all I could do. I certainly couldn't control how any woman would react to me. By keeping it real for myself, I could let them come and go and take satisfaction that at least they rejected or liked the real man that I was, complete with all my questions, torments, and objections. And my ten-minute dating rule. It also helps to expect to be ghosted.

Pooh-Poohs and Honky-Tonks

I'm a light sleeper. It's connected, I'm sure, to my father dying of a heart attack at forty-one. My brother and I were sound asleep in the room next door and never heard the ambulance arrive at midnight when he was carried away, gone forever out of our lives when he died early that morning in the hospital. Being introduced to neurotic sleep patterns at nine years old is not conducive to a lifetime of nighttime rest. A few years later, I would sit up at night waiting fretfully on the living room couch only to scurry off to bed the moment my mother pulled into the driveway. Valium and Xanax, anyone? Fortunately, my only risk is entering a twelve-step program for melatonin abuse.

Snoring is the worst. That is when *other* people snore. Though I do occasionally wake when I snore, it's usually others that put me on edge and, with little effort, can keep me there all night. My brother and I spent one painfully long night not sleeping in the living room of a house outside Munich that belonged to a U.S. Army officer who spent the night on the couch snoring so loudly that the lampshades would jingle like wind chimes. We tried to amuse ourselves by prancing around the outside patio in our underwear. Lobbying hard, we helped convince our mother that she really wasn't cut out for longterm romance with the guy.

Sleeping in a bunkhouse with twenty or more men is my version of hell. This can create bonding issues. Following my first staffing of a ManKind Project weekend workshop, I took to arriving with two handwritten posters. The first one read: "Snorers Welcome!" which I put above the door to the cabin that was farthest from where I hoped to rest. The second one read: "Non-snorers Unite!" which I placed above the door to the room where I put my sleeping bag. It didn't matter. Either there are a lot of men completely unaware of their snoring, or they can't read signs, or as "empowered men," they simply don't give a shit. As I learned, snoring is a human right.

One man accused me of "snore shaming." I didn't know that was possible. I thought snorers walked in the first rank of the unashamed and uninhibited. I longed to be like them, snoring freely, proudly, undisturbed by others, waving my sleep apnea flag high. Apparently, some (many?) men consider it an affront akin to being outed about their sexual orientation. Someone might joke about adding an S to LGBTQ for snorers, but it won't be me. I have no interest in shaming men, period. I only wanted to allow men an opportunity to self-identify so I could stay as far away from them as possible. What their bodies did when they were unconscious was my only interest. What they did when they were conscious was up to them.

Eventually, I bought a Chevy truck with an eight-foot extended bed, threw a futon in it, a camper shell on it, and parked as far away from the other men as I could and still be considered "on-site." The biggest fear I had around becoming certified to co-lead weekends was not related to performance issues leading processes, had nothing to do with moving a staff of up to fifty men toward a common goal, bore no relation to any emergency situation that all eighty-five or more men on-site might present, it pertained only to a rarely considered convention of certification: sleeping in the same cabin with the other three leaders. Earplugs, noise-canceling headphones, and sandwiching my head between two pillows was my noble attempt and repeated failure.

This now brings me to girlfriends. You'd think, "Do you snore?" might be the first question out of my mouth, but experience has shown me that even direct answers can be inconclusive. These are waters that have to be waded into gingerly. "Does penetration enhance or diminish your orgasmic potential?" is a similarly pointed question not to be asked willy-nilly. You just have to get into the ditch and start digging.

I never thought I'd fall in love with a mouth breather, but the universe demands strange things from us. My girlfriend Maggie may be the only snorer I've ever been with. She's certainly the loudest. Unless she's really tired, when she first falls asleep—which usually only takes a matter of seconds—there's a gentle plosive when the volume of air she exhales overwhelms her nasal passages and blows her lips apart with a sudden, but not overloud, "Pooh!" When I went backcountry camping with my friend Rich, I was amused and appalled to discover he made an almost identical sound. It was like I never left home. After that first night, I made sure to move my tent farther away. Friendship is best at a distance.

Maggie can pooh-pooh for quite a while. But that's on the exhale. Typically, her snoring quickly escalates to a deep, rumbling inhale. It seems to reverberate through the wind tunnel of the nose into the caverns of the sinuses until it proceeds to the back of the throat where it gets amplified into the real honk that most resembles the snoring you hear in movies. But it's more simultaneous than sequential—all the chambers and passages rattle and rumble at the same time. The quality of my night's sleep often comes down to whether it involves pooh-poohs or honky-tonks. It can affect her too. "Of course you're tired this morning. You were honky-tonking all night!"

None of this is helped by the fact that she can only sleep on her back. Because it's useless to ask her to turn on her side, I've taken to making sure she has two pillows under her head. The extra loft is god's answer to light sleepers. But the earplugs are always handy.

We now take turns videoing each other snoring. I certainly won't let her snore-shame me. Hands down, she's the worst and I have the evidence to prove it.

Fun with Diabetes

Diabetes helped me pinpoint the difference between dreaming and thinking. It's interesting because one of the first discoveries I made about meditation was the unexpected closeness between the two. This is *really* interesting, given the first film I ever made—long before I was diabetic or a meditator—was called *Dream Documentary.* You'd think I had some DNA-encoded urge to somehow reconcile the two.

I was strategizing about how to get *Dream Documentary* and my other 16mm short films shown to a theater programmer in a foreign country. This is not unusual in and of itself. But I was lying in bed at 5:00 a.m. and had just transitioned out of sleeping into thinking. Ordinarily, you wouldn't expect it to be difficult to notice the transition from unconsciousness to consciousness. Most days, it isn't. But in the middle of the night, it can be pretty subtle. "Wait a minute. I'm not dreaming. I'm thinking… I'm awake!"

I got up to check my blood sugar. Sure enough, it was low. Fifty-three. I knew it was useless to try to go back to sleep since hypoglycemia typically won't allow me that. I drank some orange juice and put on some clothes to begin this book. This was back when my wife was still alive.

She woke up and asked if I was OK, which she occasionally did when she found me awake in the middle of the night. I said yeah. But getting dressed was making more noise than I would've liked, so five minutes later she asked, "What's going on?" Rather sharply, in fact.

"I'm going to work."

"What? Now?!"

"I have an idea."

"Is your blood sugar low?"

"Not anymore."

She laughed, then went back to sleep. She knew I often did or said funny things when my blood sugar was low—also, very stupid things. I tend not to notice the difference. Though I seem to have a tendency to think whatever I say when I have hypoglycemia is brilliant, most observers might disagree. I've yet to see a single study that correlates low blood sugar with increased brain power. Increased self-deception, possibly. Decreased powers of rationality and discernment, absolutely. My distorted perceptions both added to and diminished Tracy's mirth. She knew when I had low blood sugar, I'd lost all self-diagnostic skills. This made things funnier for her. But she also tended to discount the laughs more since I wasn't trying to be funny. In her eyes, the laughs were somehow unearned. She stopped laughing with me and started laughing at me. The difference was immaterial to me but somehow, it mattered to her. I think funny's funny; any laughter is good. Who gives a shit? She wanted to know I was trying.

Part of my job was to make her laugh. This was a prime husbandly responsibility that was written into our wedding vows. "I vow to do my best to make you laugh at least once a day," we swore to each other. As with all comedy, I took it seriously. But my task was filled with more than a sense of responsibility. There was something about the way her whole body vibrated with delight. It made me happy. Along with my intentional efforts, I was pleased to take credit for the days she laughed at something stupid I'd done, which was often.

We tend to think of thinking as volitional but most of the time, it's not. Like unleashed dogs, our minds go where they want to, usually sniffing for the urine markings left by other humans or beelining it straight for their asses. It was quite an epiphany when I first realized how similar thinking was to dreaming. They have completely different reputations. Don't believe it. It's all hype. They're actually pretty close. Synapses fire and brain energy is expended. Physiologically, it's pretty much the same: mental energy. But thinking gets all the glory. Blame it on the long-standing success of educational values that put thinking above all contenders.

The major difference is that we're usually physically inert while dreaming. We're not moving around. We're sleeping. We're unconscious. That's also true when we're comatose, but not much dreaming goes on then. Then there's daydreaming. We tend not to move much then either. Yet in fact, most of what passes for thinking is not much more than daydreaming. I'm sure many philosophers and meditation instructors have written about this.

I discovered this on my first meditation retreat in 1994. Trying hard to watch my breath and stay completely present to those sensations, I spent a lot of time daydreaming. I did my best to focus my thinking, mentally saying "in" and "out" with each breath. But where I directed my mind was not where it went. At least, not for long. Like those dogs, it goes beelining after other asses. It went wherever it damn well pleased. "I wonder if the teacher ever gets foot cramps sitting like that." "Doesn't anybody want the window open for fresh air?!" "If that one neurotic woman asks another stupid question, I'm going to kill her." Oddly enough, I never experienced it as boring. I found it a worthy challenge. I still do.

Orange juice is my favorite way to deal with low blood sugar. I'm so brainwashed by my own habits that I'll think, "Oh, low blood sugar. I have no orange juice. I'm doomed." I buy three half-gallon cartons every time I go to the store. For a few years, when I felt loaded, I even got "*not* from concentrate." My observant wife accused me of over-injecting insulin to precipitate hypoglycemia. Rightly so. It's the only time I can rationalize eating sweets. I love fruit juice. Along with the sugar, I get vitamin C and hydrated too. But when I travel, I often find myself needlessly quizzing desk clerks, waiters, film festival directors, friends, and hosts whether they have any juice.

I've experienced many shameful hypoglycemic episodes on planes. I feel sheepish asking for juice before takeoff or during landings—pretty much any time before drink service starts or after it concludes. But I do it anyway. An emergency is an emergency.

Another part of me feels entitled. "Hey, I paid $110.57 for this flight. You can at least give me a few cans of juice." Fortunately, most airlines have yet to charge for it so I'll stock up. Sometimes I even take a can with me.

Do I carry other forms of glucose with me most of the time? Of course. I load up on free "fun-sized" candies every trip to the Credit Union and carry them in my backpack. I also pack glucose tabs, which qualify as over-the-counter hypoglycemia medicine. No doubt that's why I don't like them as much. Who likes taking medicine? You'd think sugar is sugar, right? No. Glucose tabs are designed to be absorbed into the bloodstream as quickly as possible and are limited to exactly four grams per tab. Eating candy at night is fine in emergencies, but the amount of sugar is not so instantly measurable or absorbable. And think of all the fat! So, at nighttime, when there's no juice available, I prefer glucose. There's something repulsive about eating M&M's at 3 a.m. Half-awake, naked on the edge of my bed, removing my mouth guard to force feed myself "real chocolate peanut candies." Or any other candy. "Choose pleasure, because just one isn't enough!" "It's more than a mouthful!" No thank you. That's the time for medicine.

My Tibetan doctor also doesn't want me to eat candy. Understandably, he doesn't want me to eat sweets, period. (If only I'd listen!) Alongside the forbidden sweets are bell peppers, sweet potatoes, yams, squash, beets, raw carrots, carrot juice, vegetable juice, pineapple, watermelon, cantaloupe, honeydew, papaya, kiwi, pears, peaches, maple syrup, coffee, and alcohol. Smoking is forbidden too. Oh, and pork. Most of the list I can understand. There's a lot of sweet stuff even in those vegetables. No smoking, alcohol, or coffee? Sure. But pork? Is he a closet Jew or a Muslim? No, he's a Tibetan monk! He was the Dalai Lama's personal physician for twenty years. Maybe before that, he was a Halal butcher. Makes you wonder what is on His Holiness' forbidden foods list.

My days of diabetes started with no insurance. It was pay-as-you-go. I did my best to reverse my disease by cutting out most carbs and exercising more than usual. The pills that I went on didn't seem to help much. My improved diet and exercise routine helped somewhat, but not enough. It wasn't long before insulin was clearly necessary. Back in 1997, it never seemed to occur to the professionals that I could be anything other than type 2. Strange, they said, for someone who was both slender and fit. And I was forty-one. By definition, I couldn't be type 1. That's childhood onset.

Wrong. Thank you, endocrinologists. The knowledge we have of this disease is still in its infancy. Going by the book, my first doctor swore I was type 2 because I contracted the disease as an adult. A later doctor swore I had to be type 1 because I quickly became insulin dependent. He assumed my diabetic condition had simply gone undiagnosed from youth, and I spent twenty-five or more years in a closeted condition. A third doctor insisted that the two known classification types are insufficient and that there needs to be a type 3 for people like me who are adult-onset but insulin dependent. He said maybe there should even be a type 4 for another unclassifiable hybrid. Nobody seemed to be looking at genetic components.

A type 1 condition seemed most likely when I examined my personal history. Hypoglycemic events were pervasive in my teens. I was ready to start grazing on the carpet before my mom would rush home from campus and say, "OK, we're going to McDonald's." Once, when I was even younger and feeling starved, she told me it was perfectly healthy to eat lawn grass. I remember stretching out in the front yard, delicately consuming a blade at a time. The flavor? A combination of weed killer, dog urine, and sandpaper. Piquant. I might've eaten three before I wised up. Wheatgrass, yes. Lawn grass, no thank you. Even at five years old, I knew she was fucking with me.

For fear of my cranky ways, close friends and family knew better than to let me go too long without eating. Now, of course, there's a word for this—hangry. When I was twenty-seven and living in Tianjin, I would come back late afternoons from six straight hours of classroom teaching and inhale candy bars and nuts just to find my equilibrium and make it until dinner. Most days, I had to lie down. Of course, a diet that consisted largely of pork, eggs, cabbage, and rice was not conducive to maintaining regular blood sugar levels.

When I was sick around Christmastime, a mere day before a scheduled long trip to the south, a Chinese friend of mine rode his bike to my bedside in the middle of the night. An expert in traditional Chinese medicine—"Western medicine makes good sense but doesn't really work. Chinese medicine makes no sense but works well,"—he diagnosed me as "not having enough strength to rest and sleep." If ever there was an equivalent Chinese description of nighttime hypoglycemia, I think that's it. I drank a nasty hot brew of molten horseshit and was on my feet and ready to travel the next morning.

By my thirties, I had a long-standing, ingrained fear of going hungry that I was only dimly conscious of. In the summer of 1991, we were filming at the Nike Basketball Camp in Princeton, NJ for *Hoop Dreams*. I went off to the bathroom. My partners Peter and Steve amused themselves by looking in the shoulder bag I'd been carrying around. There wasn't much there—some smashed cookies, a half-eaten sandwich, airplane leftovers, and a few other un-well-traveled snacks. I had become an unconscious collector of scraps. They teased me about it and had a good laugh. Though I didn't have the medical framework to articulate it at the time, the truth was those were my emergency supplies. I was afraid of low blood sugar.

Is it possible I was already diabetic in those years and just didn't know it? Did I somehow mask my diabetes with an active lifestyle and copious exercise? I don't think so. My system could never have handled all those spikes in blood sugar without also manifesting hyperglycemic symptoms: thirstiness, dehydration, frequent urination, irregular sleep patterns, weight loss, weakness, and fatigue. Still, learning I was an undiagnosed prediabetic and understanding how my poor eating habits contributed to the onset of the disease is bad enough.

I had to wait until I was forty-two before finally hitting the wall. That's probably around the exact same age my dad, had he lived, might've manifested his diabetes. For its detection, I have the high cost of film completion bonds to thank.

I was preparing for the production of my film, *The Unspoken.* Completion bonds are insurance policies that guarantee money to film investors. Should disaster occur and the film not be completed, the bondholders will reimburse investors. As most insurance policies go, they're expensive. They typically cost ten percent or more of the film's budget. My film had a budget of $500,000. Given how I was already cutting corners at every stage of production, I simply could not afford $50,000 for insurance. So I did the next best thing and took out a policy on my life.

That was a hell of a lot cheaper. I reasoned that death was the only thing that would keep me from finishing the film. Willpower is one of my gifts. But it also may have contributed to my diabetes. After all, willpower is what drove me to work long hours until I was so sapped, I practically crawled to the kitchen to stuff my face with whatever was available, catapulting me down the blood sugar roller coaster. So, I shopped for an accidental death policy for the entire production term of two years. Total cost? $4,000. Important lesson learned: my life is worth a hell of a lot less than my films.

There were just a few preliminary tests I had to take before they would grant the policy. Surprise! My A1C blood sugar test revealed a level of 7.1. Diabetics are usually defined by readings of 6.5 or higher. "No way," my girlfriend said when we got the results. She was a nutritionist working at a hospital. "It must be some kind of mistake." I figured she should know. We ordered another test. 7.0. That second test should have been the wake-up call. The jig was up. My goose was cooked. All the clichés had come home to roost. But by then, it was time to begin production. I had no time to look for another policy, assuming I could even find one that wouldn't require a similar test. My girlfriend and I didn't talk about it again for over a month. She was in shock, and I had a film to make.

In retrospect, it's a minor miracle that I was able to produce and direct the film for an entire month on location in Iowa while my blood sugar was skyrocketing out of control. I remember peeing quite a bit and being thirsty all the time, but it was an unusually hot October. I did blow up a few times. A very short temper is another warning sign for both hyper-and hypoglycemia. I was furious when my line producer pulled a bait and switch on me and took another job after the first week. Later, my entire crew threatened to walk unless I gave them raises. Once I calmed down, I realized I was better off without that Machiavellian line producer. And after I worked the numbers, I gave the crew more of a raise than they asked for. Hell, I saved all that money on my life insurance policy!

Before filming began, I arranged for the production staff on set to bring me a sandwich every three hours. In keeping with my lifelong unconscious practice, I was concerned about my blood sugar dropping low. The rational argument I made to others was that it would save time since I planned to skip lunch in order to meditate. That quickly proved unworkable because I often needed to huddle with actors, crew, or production staff during meals. I found myself eating the regularly scheduled meals as well as in between them. I also wasn't exercising. I was working twelve-hour days, six days per week. And it was stressful work, which always raises blood sugar levels. I still recall how a generous, good-hearted Grand Junction resident baked brownies and brought them to the set for one of our night shoots. I love brownies. I'm sure I ate six or seven. None of these conditions were well-suited to staving off diabetes.

When production wrapped, I was back home eating more sanely, sleeping more regularly, exercising again, and feeling like shit. Finally, my girlfriend got one of her doctor friends to see me for free and my diabetic odyssey officially began. My A1C was 14.2. You could've tapped one of my veins and used it as a coating for ice cream.

Zen Made Me OCD

I've developed my own method for unpacking boxes. Maybe it's because I've moved around so much in life. It's similar to the method I use for straightening up the house. I start by taking one object to the place it belongs. But rather than return to the starting place and repeat the process with a different object, I take whatever misplaced object I find in that second location to its proper third location. Then I pick up a misplaced object in that third location and deliver it to its new fourth location. Ad infinitum. I believe this saves time. All the time spent on those return trips back to the original source of the problem is saved. It also affords me a more free-flowing, spontaneous, creative process akin to a stream of consciousness. This way, rather than straightening one room at a time, the whole house gets straightened simultaneously in increments. If you're thinking I must have ADD, you are correct. How delusion connects to ADD, I'm not sure.

If I'm not careful, I'll structure my entire workday like this. "Gotta answer this email, gotta return this phone call, gotta run to the post office…" I have spent whole days, originally set aside for editing or writing, doing nothing more than surface events management. Problem-solving, yes, but being in a perpetual crisis mode is not a recipe for productivity. It was bad enough to have the relentless lure of phones, mail, neighbors, barking dogs, street repairs, and, most dangerously, the refrigerator. Now, of course, we live in a world gone ADD—internet, email, breaking news, online banking, tweeting…Talk about enabling!

Years ago, a friend recommended a book about ADD. "Oh yeah, baby, that's me!" I decided not to be medically diagnosed because

I thought, "What's the point?" Assuming they confirm it, they'll only recommend prescription meds, which I have no interest in. It was my girlfriend who pointed out to me I was more likely OCD. "You're not that easily distracted, but you are obsessive-compulsive. Once you get an idea in your head, you ritually have to enact it, sometimes over and over again." Compulsion typically does not leave much room for awareness. Of course, I've never bothered to have my OCD diagnosed either, but maybe my obsession with it proves I have it.

Zen made me OCD. I still remember meeting my teacher at 5 a.m. outside the *Zendo* to ceremonially hand him the incense stick that he carried to begin the morning service. He pointed out how the incense box and lighter were not aligned side by side, perfectly rectilinear with the table edges. "Order, Grasshopper, order!" Shoes in the cloakroom were disordered and robes were hanging askew. He loved pointing these things out. "Pay attention!"

When you tell people you're heading off to spend time in a Zen Buddhist Monastery, they're usually jealous. They assume you'll have an experience akin to vacationing at a spa or taking a workshop at a retreat center. They don't envision you waking up at 4:30 a.m. every day, chanting, meditating, and working hard until 10:00 p.m. when you gratefully fall into bed. They don't envision you down on your hands and knees scrubbing floors with a wet rag, cleaning toilets, vacuuming cushions, and scouring pots. While making the beds, the pillows must be plumped and placed just so, and the corners of the sheets and blankets folded precisely. It's OCD paradise. Now when I enter the house and remove my shoes, I tend to line them perfectly along the staircase wall.

At one level, the purpose of Zen practice is to stay fully aware, moment to moment, about everything going on inside and outside the body—becoming a field of pure awareness. Very easy to explain, not so easy to do. That's why we meditate. We practice. Practice to prepare for when we're *not* sitting on a comfortable cushion in a quiet room listening to the birds outside. Practice for when our children suddenly disappear, our boss fires us, the FBI knocks at the front door, or our wife is dying…practice for the whole of the rest of life, all the vicissitudes and all the joys. "The full catastrophe!" as Zorba the Greek put it.

Everyone has their own unique impediments to practice. Most involve learning to sit down and shut up so we can maintain that internal stillness during the daily onslaught of life's challenges and indignities. I'm not entirely sure why, but I tend toward calm during moments of extreme life drama and circumstances like those above. But less extreme drama, those daily vicissitudes? That's when I give vent to quick frustration. The smallest, most commonplace things can piss me off. Yes, I'm talking about dealing with the post office. And talking to the cable company about bad service, getting the bank to fix their mistakes, settling an insurance claim, finding that my emails are suddenly no longer delivered, not being able to open a molded plastic package of headphones, or spilling uncooked spaghetti all over the floor…The list is long, and those are only a few commonplace frustrations. The most frustrating of all is to wake up at sixty-seven and find you've become a curmudgeon.

Yes, I get angry at the smallest things. At even smaller things, I may not get angry, but I have little patience. The quotidian has been my historical enemy. I have little forbearance for dusting the furniture, changing light bulbs, shopping for groceries, taking out the trash, and doing the laundry. What's the point of having patience? They're goddamn chores that bear no intrinsic interest, they just have to get done. They're small potatoes, right? All the boring shit you have to do to sustain life. Isn't that the rule? In order to enjoy the good stuff later, you have to go through all the small stuff. The Cartesian worldview. Manichean even.

But what if the small stuff isn't the enemy? What if the trivialities of daily life are not just shit we have to wade through to get to the goodies? What if there are just as many goodies in the small stuff? This might be the world's biggest and best-kept secret. It might be life's secret cookie jar. Since I'm a cookie addict, I want in!

Can we actually train our minds to appreciate the small stuff, develop forbearance and patience, and develop strategies for not flying off the handle? How do we maintain those qualities that meditation helps us practice—that awareness, that equilibrium—during our day-to-day? How do we slow down enough to begin to experience that? Ironically, and perhaps paradoxically, we do it by actually staying present with all that small stuff. By not letting our minds run away with any of the bigger stuff. For me, that means maintaining my focus squarely on the small stuff. As John Lennon said, "Life is what happens to you when you're busy making other plans."

I take out the trash, wash the dishes, shop for groceries, and change light bulbs, all the while doing my best to stay focused on each task. I'll often say to myself, "I'm taking out the trash, I'm washing the dishes, I'm shopping for groceries, I'm changing light bulbs." I'll narrate what I'm doing while I'm doing it. Sometimes, I'll also say to myself, "This could be the most important thing I do today." (Most of the time, it isn't, but you never know. My days can be pretty goddamn boring. It's important to proceed "as if.") It serves as a very good reminder. "This is my life! Live it now! This could be the very moment of my awakening!"

There's a famous account of the Buddha giving a talk on Vulture Peak to his assembled monks; he didn't say a word but simply held up a flower. It is said that the disciple Mahākāśyapa awakened at that moment. Any action, at any time, can be an impetus to awaken, no matter how lowly or exalted. "Yes, right now, while I'm taking a shit!" Clearly, not all actions are deemed equal. Not all actions are given their proper due or recognized as a moment of potential awakening. But they should be! Who knows how many people have spontaneously awakened washing dishes? If I ever achieve enlightenment while cleaning up spilled spaghetti from the floor, I'll be well-rehearsed. If every moment of our lives is valuable and precious, then every moment also represents potential enlightenment.

This is all wonderful and good, but there's only one problem. This is not Zen! The purpose of Zen is not so you can "sing along" in your head, narrating what you're doing. "I am walking the dog. I am watching him pee on a tree. I am looking at him sniff another dog's ass." No. It is to experience those things fully in and of themselves, not to transcribe them into a stream-of-consciousness archive.

The purpose is also not to "empty your mind of all thoughts." So many misguided teachers of mindfulness and yoga commonly teach this. You cannot empty your mind of all thoughts! Won't happen! You can slow them down, but you can't get rid of them. A study with some of the most advanced meditators in India determined that the longest anyone can reasonably go without a thought in their head is about fifteen seconds. This should not be a surprise. The purpose of the mind is to create thought, no less than the purpose of the heart is to pump blood. That's its job. Its reason for being. Hell, the brain works so well it doesn't even cease immediately upon death. Studies have shown that the deceased can show signs of mental activity an hour or more after death. That's part of why it's very difficult to determine the actual moment of death. The mind makes it elusive and tricky. The heart may have stopped and breathing may have ceased, but the mind may still be functioning. "Oh shit, I forgot to take out the trash!" We can hope that won't be our final thought, but you never know. As we say in Zen, "The thought of no-thought is thought."

The objective is not the cessation of thought. It's simply (but not easily) to be completely *unattached* to thought. The aim is to make any thought that arises no more than a passing interest. Aim to make it no more significant than anything else you're seeing, hearing, smelling, touching, or tasting. The metaphor that's commonly used is like clouds flitting across the sky or like ripples of water floating downstream. As soon as a given thought hooks us, "Oh, I'm sure he doesn't really like me," then typically, we're already out of touch with what else is actually occurring and we're lost in the slipstream of mind.

Order is one thing. But my OCD takes me to some interesting places. And by "interesting," I mean boring. Watch and observe what a man with too much time on his hands and unharnessed brain power can succumb to. I'll come home after an afternoon swim, walk in the front door, and immediately begin an interior dialogue. "Should I hook my backpack on to the closet handle or just rest it on the bench? I don't want to forget to refill my traveling glucose container. Should I do that before I hang up my swimsuit or after? Better do it now or else I'll forget. But first I need to slip off my Crocs and put on my slippers. Or should I hang up my jacket? Will it be easier to take the groceries to the staircase on my way to the bedroom to fill up my glucose, or should I double back and get them later? Eventually, I'll need to return the bags to the car. So maybe I should empty them now, carry all the groceries upstairs separately, and leave the bag here." I'll get my head so wrapped up in knots that I'll end up dropping all the groceries—which have been overflowing from my arms this whole time—onto the bed in order to free my hands to fill up my glucose container.

Then I'll go back to the hallway to pick up the empty bags to fill them with the groceries now splayed across my bed so I can carry them upstairs! This is just a sample of the nonsense that goes through my head all the time. Rather than tell people, "That store is four or five blocks away," I'll walk the route in my head and count them just to arrive at the exact number.

This is not Zen. This is neurosis! This is extreme self-consciousness. This is OCD! As far as I can tell, it's not good for anything. Another fine way to define Zen is "flow." You want to flow from one moment to another without a backward glance, worry, or self-doubt and be at ease with all that presents itself. You want to have absolute confidence that whatever decision you make, action you take, or circumstance you encounter, they're all perfect in their own way. That's why I sometimes tell people that the fulfillment of Zen is not achieving some goal outside yourself or some template of impeccable behavior. It's becoming the most full, complete, comfortable, and secure version of yourself. It's you being you. But with a lighthearted ease, a joyous and expansive mind, and an openhearted acceptance. Not with manic self-consciousness. That is what lies in wait deep within each of us. That is our Buddha nature. We just need to include and transcend all the neuroses and OCD that bubbles perpetually on the surface. So do as I say, not as I do!

The good news for me is that even though there's no progress to make and there's nothing to get better at, I'm making progress and getting better at things. You know how I know? I just enjoy doing simple things more. I do all those little things that need to be done with more acceptance and ease, even joy. I enjoy taking out the trash now; it gives me a chance to get outside and feel the air and the sun. I like washing the dishes, especially in winter, because it's a chance to warm up my freezing hands. I love the smell and warm feel of pulling fresh laundry from the dryer. I like putting clean sheets on the bed. And now that I know how to properly secure the quilt inside its cover, I no longer live in fear. For me, it's not the hokey-pokey; tying my shoes might actually be what my life is all about.

This tendency has only increased since the arrival of Covid. There's less to do and more time to do it in. Along with my typical busyness, many aspirations of achievement have dissolved into the ether. I no longer have that voice in my head telling me, "You should be accepting an Academy Award at the Oscars, not rearranging socks in your drawer." "I bet Bob Dylan never takes out the garbage." "Adding additional wire hangers to my closet will never get me on *Fresh Air* with Terry Gross." That urgency to "do more; do it now; do it faster" seems to have left my system like sweat evaporating off skin in the warm sunshine. I may have lost a lot of drive, but the few places I'm going are certainly more enjoyable.

I sometimes still narrate what I'm doing to myself, but I've turned it into a game. I'll do it with the tongue-in-cheek voice of a stern father. When I pull up my pants and cinch my belt, I say out loud, "Pull up your pants, son! You look like a clown at the circus." Or when putting laundry away, "Fold your clothes properly, son! Your mother's not here to do it for ya." Yes, it's always "son" I'm talking to. Is it my own father's voice, transported over sixty years, resurrected from the grave? Maybe. But it's also, if not only, my own "fatherly" voice gently chiding the youngster within to not be lazy and do the right thing. Learning to father ourselves may well be the final rung on the ladder of Mature Masculinity. Doing it with a chuckle makes the climb that much more enjoyable.

Every morning I get up and open the blinds, curious about the light outside. Is it sunny? Cloudy? What's out there? How might it impact what I have planned today? I like walking into the room later in the day and seeing the light pour through the windows. Every evening I close them. I do this over and over, day in, day out. What for? I used to think it was a waste of time. Isn't it less effort, simpler, and more efficient to just keep them closed all the time? Yes, it is. But is that the greatest value? Is efficiency my life's highest priority? Maybe it was once. It now appears to be changing. Making an effort now seems more about doing for the sake of doing and seeing for the sake of seeing. We tend to repeat "useless" patterns as human beings. Somehow that seems to be the stuff of life. We do it because we do it. Circular causation. But isn't there a unique flavor to each different doing? A unique feeling, or maybe even piquancy? It seems to me there is, and I relish it, whether or not I decide to sing, half-mockingly and half-adoringly, occasional verses of "Sunrise, Sunset."

In the past, while idling at a long stoplight, standing in line at the grocery, or waiting for a ride on a street corner, I would reach for my cell phone. Now I don't do that. I just breathe, relax, and drop further into the moment. Nothing to do, nowhere to go. Just being. Sometimes I consciously meditate, eyes open. More often, it's just a reflex—breathe, look around, see what's happening. I get a hell of a lot less done, no question. But I'm happier. Taking naps has become the highlight of my day. I also take time to read more. And I watch the Golden State Warriors without worrying whether I should be more productive and start a new screenplay. I don't get caught in fear that I'm wasting my life because basketball has become an addiction. Some nights, I recognize that meditating was the most important thing I did all day. Sometimes, I do wonder if I won't be the best-rested man to ever arrive at death. Maybe I'll be so relaxed I won't notice the difference.

But have no fear, I'm still a curmudgeon. I still get cranky dealing with the bank, the internet company, the post office, and insurance agents. Though I always do my best not to snap at clerks, it's a challenge when I invariably ask them questions outside their script. "What do you mean it's not your policy to help customers with that problem?" "Why do you have to transfer me to another department where I'll wait on hold for another thirty minutes?!" I know there's a human being in there somewhere! One with her own Buddha nature.

Now I accept myself for the curmudgeon I am and don't get too hung up on trying to be different.

Pornography Returns to China

It was not my intention, but I might have reintroduced pornography to mainland China.

Friends and I were walking down a somewhat deserted late-night Hong Kong street. I was on vacation. A bus passed, and suddenly, a VHS tape skidded to a stop right in front of me. It had no case and was unlabeled. I picked it up and ran after the bus, now waiting at a stoplight. I held up the tape and waved it. I was sure someone had dropped it. The few passengers looked at me blankly. I'm sure they thought I was deranged. Maybe someone purposely threw it out the window. Clearly, no one recognized it, wanted it, or wanted anything to do with me. The bus drove on and I thought, "Somehow, I'm meant to have this."

I played the tape when I got back to my Beijing apartment a week later, and sure enough, it was porn. Before I went through mainland customs, I figured if they found it and played it, I could claim ignorance since I had no idea what it was. But I already suspected it might be porn and it wasn't lost on me how severe the penalties were at that time for porn smugglers. For Chinese citizens, possibly execution. For foreigners, likely deportation.

Deportation? That was a risk I was willing to take.

It was the winter of 1984. I already had a year's experience crossing the border, going in and out of Chinese customs. When I first arrived in August 1983, I purposely did not bring my 16mm Bolex camera with me. Customs regulations were clear. I knew because I checked them with the Chinese consulate. They considered 16mm film professional filmmaking gear and required lengthy forms and explanations as to what you were filming and why. I had every intention of making a professional film based on my two years living there, but I had no intention of telling authorities what I was filming and why. I brought only high-quality "amateur" gear, figuring I'd blow up the image in post or, as they say today, "up-res it." In practice, border agents at the time couldn't tell the difference between cameras taking 35mm photographs or movie film gauged 16mm, 35mm, or Super 8, or likely, a fly fishing rod. Their education in the infinite variety of consumer goods from the West was limited.

Videotape they knew. Somewhat. As a so-called "foreign expert," I had finagled a VHS tape player from my department at the university for use in my apartment. Formerly called the Foreign Trade Institute, the brand-new University of International Business and Economics took an ambitious step forward in 1984 when it changed its name. My job there entailed educating colleagues in some of the latest Western video production techniques. Japan's Sony Corporation had gifted the Institute a million-dollar TV studio. Though modest by U.S. commercial standards, it was a fully equipped studio any small U.S. public access station would have been proud to own. I viewed it as my personal playground. I was entrusted to produce whatever I saw fit. Given that every video the school produced prior to my arrival meant turning on a camera when someone was teaching a class or making a speech, I didn't have to work hard to add sophistication. But my directorial marvels only started rolling out of the studio mid-year. These were the very early days of China's "economic miracle," and when I arrived in August, construction was not yet complete. The sound mixing board sat under sheets of plastic covered in plaster dust. On that same campus tour, I was also shown the university's one and only computer. A main frame behemoth—also shrouded in sheets of plastic—sat alone and unplugged in a separate room. Clearly, it hadn't been used and wasn't going to be any time soon. I wasn't going to let that happen to the studio. It's in my nature to be productive.

I was given a large office with a modest desk, chair, and a tiny electric heater. Not a lick of other furniture. The building had no central heating or cooling. Come winter—which indoors, began in October—and gripped by fear of setting new cold stress index records, I needed to find something to occupy my time. Feeling forgotten in my office, huddled over endless cups of hot tea, there were only so many books and magazines I could stand to waste my time with. So, I took to writing the first-ever English card catalog for the university's video library. Down in the vault where the tapes were stored and, as far as I could tell, almost never accessed, with my fingerless gloves, six layers of long underwear, sweaters, and jackets, I banged out five hundred fifty entries by hand on a 1939 Smith Corona typewriter—one for each tape. That's when I first got the notion to borrow a tape deck.

I could take tapes home to actually enjoy watching them while maintaining a body temperature close to 98.6 degrees.

The collection was eclectic with programming produced in at least twenty-five countries. Many of the productions were Russian, although the BBC was well-represented. Regardless of the original language, the tapes were often dubbed into a second language and subtitled in as many as two more languages. The print of the 1966 Russian version of *War and Peace* might well have been dubbed into Danish with subtitles in Dutch and Chinese. It was impossible to know how the tapes got into the collection and under what provenance. Most were three-quarter-inch U-Matics and likely started arriving in 1976 after the Cultural Revolution ended. In the spirit of the times—"*man man zou,*" a Beijing colloquialism meaning "take it easy"—I took to watching whole hour-long episodes before typing in seven or eight small bits of information on three-by-five-inch index cards. There were more than a few gems. Most were based on literary classics I had never seen before. I was delighted to watch them, if not in their entirety, then at least partially since my Protestant work ethic regularly got the better of me. I felt guilty watching hour after hour of Chekov's oeuvre. Since I recall maybe three people showing up to check out a tape during the entirety of my three-month mission, I don't think my equally frozen colleagues, spending their days sipping tea, eating sunflower seeds, and chatting, were overly concerned.

I liked my boss, Mr. Ding. He spent two years studying for an MA in Canada, so his English was good. My Chinese, despite a summer course and private lessons the year before, was largely suitable for ordering dumplings and getting the "soft cushion seats" on trains. (Because China was nominally a classless society, they didn't call them "first class" tickets.) My favorite studio colleague and confidant, Mr. Jing, spoke passable English and was also close to me in age. He became my primary translator. Other colleagues were all much older and spoke little to no English. Despite giving them all lessons in English camera terminology and broadcast studio techniques, live-to-tape filming proved challenging. Directions called out through my headset to camera operators invariably went awry. If I asked for a slow zoom out, I might get a pan right, and the camera would stare off into empty space—a sudden existential contemplation of darkness. When I asked for a close-up, I might get a tilt up to the ceiling. "Anyone up there?" Seeing the mistakes, Mr. Jing would yell out the correct Chinese term, but the momentary opportunity had usually passed and we would cut back just as someone lapsed into complete silence, coughed, or blew their nose.

I was working the Chinese system long before I knew how the Chinese system worked. I received the UIBE offer thanks to time-tested Chinese channels: *"zǒu hòu mén"*—"through the back door." I wanted to spend a second year in China following my first in Tianjin, partly to be with my Finnish girlfriend who was studying there for another year. I put the word out that I was looking for a job. I was hoping not to have to teach ESL again. I wanted to do what I was actually trained to do. A Chinese friend of mine asked around and came up with the UIBE offer. The only stipulation, which I readily agreed to, was to not make waves about my pay grade and title. I was to be a "foreign instructor," not a "foreign expert," and was accordingly paid less.

It took me only five months to betray her. I didn't care much about the money. But reduced fringe benefits, not being included on events and trips with my foreign colleagues, and receiving less professional respect, was painful. They were called "Professor." I was "Mr. Marx." So yes, partly it was my ego. OK, more money was good too.

I solicited the support of my "grand teacher," George Semsel. I called him my grand teacher because he was professor to my film-making professor, Mike Covell. George was the head of Mike's MFA thesis committee, and Mike was the head of mine. George had landed a one-year position at *You-Yi Binguan* (Friendship Hotel)—where I was living at the time—with the aptly named China Film Censorship and Propaganda Bureau. His job was to review foreign and domestic films and help his colleagues understand what they actually meant. I believe it was George who informed his colleagues they might want to change the English name used for the Chinese equivalent of the Oscars. We had quite a few laughs during the yearly "Golden Cock Awards."

We quickly became friends. George graciously wrote a letter explaining how, in the U.S., the MFA is considered a "terminal degree" equivalent to a PhD, accrediting artists for university faculty positions. Addressed "To Whom It May Concern," I promptly dropped the letter on Mr. Ding's desk. Though he later upped my salary and status, he was unhappy with my insubordination. It wouldn't be the last time.

My pornographic treasure started making the rounds at *You-Yi*. I mentioned to one or two friends that I was sitting on valuable contraband and that was all it took. I was besieged by offers. Built to house Soviet experts in the 1950s who arrived to help China build their own socialist paradise, the sprawling, multi-building compound in northwest Beijing became home to as many as one thousand doctors, lawyers, engineers, scientists, and teachers. In the early 1960s, China and the USSR had a falling out and the Russians left, freeing up a lot of rooms for visiting academics and Communist Party refugees from around the world. For me, it was paradise. I was given a large flat, housecleaning services, access to the compound's post office, convenience store, restaurants, swimming pool, and tennis and basketball courts. My favorite restaurant, unforgettably named Dining Hall #7, was mere steps from my apartment. Every night featured brilliant minds seated at open tables, buzzing about world affairs in at least twenty different languages.

I was living in a country club for exiled intellectuals: refugees from the 1965-66 Indonesian genocide and the beginning of the Suharto dictatorship, 1950s McCarthyism, Chilean refugees from Pinochet... By ones and twos, they came from around the world to be welcomed by the Chinese, an influx only partly slowed by their own ten-year purge during the Cultural Revolution. In addition to the permanent residents, there was a revolving door of visiting journalists, artists, and scholars who came for days or weeks. That was where I first saw Alan Ginsburg, Maxine Hong Kingston, and Toni Morrison. Most of the foreign experts were there for a year or more. I was a twenty-eight-year-old filmmaker with a recently minted MFA and few job prospects in the U.S. I couldn't believe my good fortune.

When it comes to prurience, leftists and intellectuals are pretty much like everyone else. I had to limit the tape's checkout policy to one week. More than a few neighborhood relationships experienced a renewed sex drive. Taking their inspiration from our Chinese hosts, who were not signatories to any international trade agreements and observed no copyright laws, people made their own copies. That helped ease the demand. I don't know what the appeal was. I watched it a few times with my girlfriend. It certainly had an erotic impact, but like all pornography, too much too quickly became deadening. Was the appeal forbidden fruit? The fact that it was dangerously illegal? "Sticking it to The Man"? Reconnecting with the pleasures of home? These were the old days before porn was ubiquitous and free. I cannot recall a single image from the tape, which is remarkable given that my memory for film images is usually impeccable.

In May of 1985, I started preparing to leave China for good. I was ready to go. Working at UIBE was great for my resume, but I wanted to stalk bigger filmmaking fish back home. I planned to take the Trans-Siberian Express from Beijing to Moscow, go to Helsinki with my girlfriend, see a few friends in Europe, then head home. I had no intention of taking the tape with me. Or at least its contents. On one of my last days on campus, I handed it to Mrs. Wang, one of my colleagues at the studio, and asked her to use it to copy the programs I'd produced for the school. I'm a firm believer in recycling.

When I came in the next day, Mr. Jing met me outside the door. "I need to talk to you." Immediately, I sensed the worst had occurred. He steered me away from the studio.

"After you left, Mr. Ding came through the studio with a group of visiting dignitaries." At that point, I knew I was wrong. It was worse than the worst.

"He showed them around, then wanted to present our seven-minute 'Welcome to UIBE!' video." Mr. Ding was rightly proud of that show. So was I. It was a solid PR video the university could use for various future occasions, introducing visiting dignitaries to the school and setting it apart from institutions less technically and promotionally savvy. It was my parting gift. It would help raise UIBE's domestic and international standings. It was my directorial debut in the competitive field of low-end video production with a future soon to entail children's birthday parties and bar mitzvahs.

"He asked to see the program, but for some reason, the three-quarter-inch master wasn't available. Mrs. Wang said the dub she made for you was still in the VHS machine. Mr. Ding said, 'That'll be fine,' and off they went. Everyone loved it. But then the program ended and the pornography started."

This was bad. Worse than bad. Catastrophic. What kind of a shit-storm had I set off? I was terrified. Though just as quickly, I was somewhat reassured by Mr. Jing. More than his words, I remember his manner. He was amused.

His demeanor said, "I don't think it's going to be a big deal. We're not reserving seats on a one-way train to a Chinese gulag."

An hour later, Mr. Ding paid me a rare office visit. I did my best to point out that the tape was like a classroom blackboard—you could use it to work on physics theorems or you could draw lewd pictures on it. The tape itself was less of an issue than its content. It was a diversionary tactic. I don't recall making it clear that I should have done the responsible thing and bulk-erased the tape before handing it to Mrs. Wang. He inquired about its provenance. I recounted my fateful encounter on a deserted Hong Kong street. Mr. Ding might have been inexperienced about many things related to film and video production, but he was not stupid. He thought it preposterous. I'm a professional storyteller, and I thought so too. There's nothing quite like that feeling of telling someone exactly what happened to you when it sounds like complete bullshit to your own ears. Naturally, he assumed I was lying. Yet there it was. It happened. I could hear the wheels whirring in his head. "What should I do with this lying jackass who could get us all sent to the countryside to feed pigs for the rest of our lives?" Though I can't say that this particular incident was seminal, certain events like this throughout my life account for why I make documentaries and write non-fiction books. Reality tends to be crazier than fiction.

If word got out that the UIBE video production studio owned, much less *produced* a porn tape, the repercussions would have been cataclysmic. I would've been put on the next plane home. But my colleagues could've been shipped off to shovel horseshit on a communal farm in the countryside for years. Certainly, that would have been the case a few years earlier during the Cultural Revolution. Or it could have meant prison. The studio would likely have been shut down forever.

As far as I know, word never leaked to Communist Party authorities. On the face of it, this is a miracle. Everyone, whether in the party or not, is encouraged to report on everyone else. It can mean a significant reward for the whistleblowers. But rather than a miracle, maybe it's more a logical, albeit paradoxical, function of that very same Chinese Communist Party culture. When things go wrong, *everyone* is at risk. Everyone can be implicated. Certainly Mrs. Wang, Mr. Jing, my other colleagues at the studio, and perhaps especially Mr. Ding, the man in charge, but even the visiting dignitaries who were innocent bystanders, all could have been swept up in a wave of repercussions. Truthfully, they were all innocent bystanders. None of them knew what was on that tape, including Mrs. Wang, who presumably never bothered to look before she pressed record. But if even one of them blew the whistle, they would all be forever tarred by association and rife for lifelong retribution. Everyone involved took the only possible course—forget it ever happened. Unsee it and never speak a word about it again. It was the Chinese thing to do.

Since I ended up putting ten people's livelihoods and futures at risk, I accepted some meager responsibility. I confessed to Mr. Ding how senseless it was for me to bring the tape across the border back to Beijing. I like to think the whole episode contributed to my present-day accountability standards of accepting the impacts seen and unseen for all my actions, conscious or unconscious. But self-rationalization is a slippery slope. As I often have in my life, I did something really stupid. My devil-may-care attitude is imprecise. The devil does care, and he can make you pay for being a moron. Fortunately for Mr. Ding, he knew in a week he'd be rid of me forever. Looking back now, my second, far smaller regret is that I didn't buy him a bottle of Maotai (China's famous distilled liquor) as a parting gift. He could have toasted my departure. Unlike him and all my colleagues, only I had the rare privilege of ever sharing the story, which I repeatedly did with my friends at You-Yi before I left, with great hilarity.

Adventures with Poison Oak

Though my late wife and I nurtured each other regularly through sickness and health, no episode stands out more to me than when I got poison oak on our first road trip together in the summer of 2003. This was before we were married, only six months after we met. We were visiting her daughter in Eugene, Oregon, truck camping in the "white palace"—my all-white Chevy 1500 WT. Complete with an eight-foot extended bed, a camper shell, and a permanently installed queen-sized futon in the back, we could drop anchor anywhere, crawl in the back, and sleep like royalty. Add a couple of bikes and a cooler, and we could hit the road for days, and we did—Yosemite, Lake Tahoe, Big Sur, Redwood National Forest, Mendocino, Mt. Lassen, Mt. Shasta—most of those places on this one trip.

I headed out jogging from her daughter's house one morning. I used to love exploring neighborhoods that way. Her place was semi-rural, so I was enjoying the back roads on an early summer day. Before long, I needed to take a crap. I hate when that happens. Usually, I'll wait until I've had a bowel movement before taking off, but this morning I forgot. The country was wide open, but I found a large shaded yard, shielded from both street and house by large trees. A nice green spot with lots of little plants. You know where this is going...

Being from the Midwest, I was quite familiar with poison ivy, but not so much with poison oak. I tore off handfuls of it to wipe myself clean and happily resumed my run. It took about two days for things to start getting uncomfortable. We were driving the Columbia River Gorge. I could barely sit still. Finally, it dawned on me what I'd done. We pulled into a rest stop and commandeered a bathroom. I dropped my trousers, bent over, and spread my legs for Tracy to take a look. This is not what I recommend to young couples for building intimacy. She confirmed the worst. After she straightened up from being doubled over from laughter, she was extremely sympathetic. When I wasn't sitting in oatmeal baths, I spent much of the next ten days having Tracy apply various ointments to my inflamed butt cheeks and painfully aggrieved anus. Though she was an able mother after raising two daughters, receiving that kind of care from her was not how I wanted to ramp up our romantic life. It made a great story to tell at diverse social gatherings. Aside from gaining a deep appreciation for what poison oak looks like, I vowed never to go jogging without an ample supply of toilet paper.

The Hilarity of Depression

People tend to overlook how funny depression is. I should know. I've been depressed a lot.

Everybody is trying to find their own way out of this bag of skin and bones, neurotransmitters, and thought patterns handed to them at birth. It's painful, this thing called life. The Buddha pointed that out four thousand years ago, but nobody seems to be paying much attention. Everybody wants to be born again—a yoga master, a Tony Robbins success story, the next great talk show host, or at least a porn star—to transcend this earthly frame of earwax, heartbreak, corns, and betrayal. Drugs, meditation, dharma study, men's work, therapy, exercise, and more have not eased the pain of never achieving supereminence.

They say that a minority of depression cases can be caused by genetics. The vast majority of cases are due to environmental factors like adverse childhood events (ACE), drug and alcohol abuse or other forms of addiction, losing a loved one, or having health issues. I've pretty much tried them all and I must admit, for me, it's something different. For me, it's due to ineffectiveness—the inability to impose my will upon the world.

Feeling impotent? *That*, I've experienced a lot.

Ever try to get people to do what you want? I have. I keep trying all the time. I never learn. When I can afford it, I enjoy *paying* people to do what I want. (It's rare, but it does happen.) But even people that I pay won't necessarily do what I want. If this happens often enough and my best intentions are thwarted, what is the result? Depression.

It often seems like anything I do, or try to do, makes no difference. The old adage is true: "When man makes plans, God laughs." I'm confident I've kept God in stitches for years. The Exalted One must be having a nonstop comedy telethon, complete with celebrity guests, musical dance numbers, and sitcom sketches. The passing parade of incompetence, inefficiency, misunderstanding, mistaken beliefs, and downright stupidity, not to mention all the "-isms"—sexism, racism, classism, ageism, ableism, narcissism—all the structured cultural and institutional ways ignorance gets perpetuated, well, let's just say it makes patience difficult. Move over equanimity. Welcome exasperation!

Exhausted patience is one thing. What about when you feel like life isn't worth living? That's my default setting. Somehow, somewhere in my childhood, I got the memo quoting the wrong rule book. Instead of, "Do your best, and let things happen as they will," I got the memo that said, "Do your best, and if you can't make things happen as they should, you are a complete fuck-up." Sure, it's easy to say, "Oh, that's just narcissism coupled with a strong self-critic." Of course it is. And what's your point? An awareness of that doesn't mean that I will suddenly stop trying to effect change and sing kumbaya because I've now learned that expecting results is futile. I quickly default to the bottom line: "What's the use? Fuck it…" My inclination, all too readily at hand, is to give up. I don't need an emotional support dog. Despair is my best friend.

Truly and deeply accepting the futility of expecting results may be fine for attaining enlightenment. (I've made that connection a few times, and believe me, the resulting joy actually feels like enlightenment.) It's at least good for establishing the basis for equanimity in life. But that kind of acceptance can easily lead to resignation, which in turn can lead to nihilism. The judgment that human beings are useless and should be trusted for nothing is common for me. At my most despairing, I'll say, "People are fools suitable only to become blind followers." Sounds like the Vladimir Putin School of Governance. John

Lennon famously said, "You want to save humanity. But it's people that you just can't stand." Guilty! Establishing that precedent is also conducive to living life as a hedonist, immersing yourself in all the earthly pleasures and accomplishing little more than establishing eligibility for multiple memberships in twelve-step programs. I've considered that life path, and despite its occasional allure, I keep opting for less cynical choices. Despair may be my best friend, but he is not my pilot.

I'm caught between two hard places. I'm perpetually drawn to despair and giving up, but I can't accept that choice because I find it morally bankrupt and aesthetically dull. What's an unrepentant rebel to do?

You could start by sitting down and compiling a list of all the things you tried to do and failed at. I have, and it's a long one. I wrote it once, but who really needed to? I committed it to memory long ago, constantly updating it as needed. Typically, when I'm supposed to be meditating in the morning, I'll mentally run through that list and revisit some of the best selections. That is, the best of the worst. It brings new meaning to the phrase "top-ten hits."

Isn't that an element of depression? Where you can't get unstuck from the grooves of a song playing over and over again? A song that has a familiar chorus where only the names of the perpetrators change?

"He fucked me.

She fucked me.

They fucked me.

Fuck them!

Fuck me!"

Catchy, isn't it? I know that song and I've sung every possible variation. Let's face it. It is popular. I once visited an old friend while he was reworking his own greatest hits. I found him banging his head against the living room wall. When his wife and kids would try to stop him, he'd hit them. Frozen in time and rehashing the key mistakes of his life, he was having a nervous breakdown. What was odd was that he could be perfectly rational and have a reasonably lucid conversation one moment, then when he followed the logic of his own mind back to how he screwed up, he resumed his hard rock thrashing. Perhaps he was literally trying to knock the thoughts out of his head. They say that electroshock can be extremely effective at times like this and I believe them. Reboot the brain. Overload the voltage firing the same old synapses and blow them out. Fortunately, it's never come to that for me. I've opted for a less dramatic reset—meditation. It's cheaper. Though it does eat up a lot of time. I'll likely overdo it and end up a charter member of Meditators Anonymous.

I figure this separates the merely depressed from the terminally insane. The merely depressed may still have the capacity to say to themselves, "Here we go again. I can ride this cesspool of despair down into the sewer, or I can choose to get help of some kind." The terminally insane may be unable to leave the cesspool.

Boredom is what saved me. I get bored running the same old hits again. Feeling the same shitty way all the shitty time about the same old shit finally motivated me to do other things. They say boredom is the worst fear for those who have ADD and ADHD. What they don't tell you is that it may save your life. Though it's not a headline you see often, it's honestly true for me, "Boredom Saved My Life!" I can't stand doing the same thing over and over again, even grousing and feeling miserable. I can't even stand making films the same way I made them before or making them about the same subjects. I can't stand repeating myself in conversation, either. Listen closely. Once I've said it, that's all you get. I'm one and done. Maybe that's what makes artists artists. They hate repeating themselves.

I realize it's not that easy for most people with depression. You can get locked in and feel like there's no way out. Having the ability to choose makes me an anomaly. But what if it didn't? What if, at some level, all of us who are not mentally impaired have the opportunity to choose? What if there's a junction we all come to that points in two different directions? "Turn here to live a life of happiness and fulfill-ment. Turn here to live a life of frustration and angst." My genetic inheritance told me to walk through that second door. Nobody in their right mind will choose door number two. Yet that's exactly what we do over and over again. Rather than focus on what's good and working in my life right now, I'm going to focus on those fucks who screwed me over. "Fuck them! I'll get revenge!"

In the pantheon of Buddhist teachings, the ancient Pali word *dukkha* gets translated many different ways. "Suffering" is the most common. Hence, the Buddha's First Noble Truth is usually stated as, "Suffering is an undeniable fact of existence." It's a fact of life, living causes pain. But *dukkha* can also be translated as "unsatisfactori-ness." "*This* isn't good enough. *That* isn't good enough. Nothing is good enough!" Can you relate to that? I can. Nothing is sufficient; everything is somehow wanting. It's a terrible way to live, yet that's exactly how many of us do it. "If I only had more_____, I'd be happy!" "He who dies with the most toys wins." "The more you spend, the more you save!" We're hosed by advertising slogans and flushed by a consumerist culture that promotes unsatisfactoriness.

Both of the monks who starred in my film *Journey from Zanskar* are exemplary for not living in *dukkha*. Again and again, they don't pray for success for themselves or their mission, they pray for the happiness and well-being of all beings. What's the point of lifting just my own boat? Especially when, much of the time, it proves impos-sible. Why not lift all boats? I know of no better cure for depression than getting out into the world and acting in service to other people. If nothing else, you'll quickly realize, "Jeez, so many people have it far worse than I do." It's the secret code of life. If seeing other people in pain doesn't cheer you up, nothing will!

Aging and the Decline of the Human Body

> I asked [Dr. Felix] Silverstone whether gerontologists have discerned any particular, reproducible pathway to aging. "No," he said. "We just fall apart."
> Atul Gawande, *Being Mortal. Picador, page 35.*

I don't understand what's happened to my pee stream. It's like the urine, having made its way down the urethra to the head of my penis, suddenly becomes confused, unsure which way to turn. Left? Right? Why not make a U-turn?

What the hell happened?! Where did this uncertainty come from? Is there a construction zone ahead? Some road hazard? Whatever happened to going straight? (Or "going forward," as my brother told me to say thirty years ago so as not to offend gay and queer friends.)

I can point my penis in an unmistakably clear direction right into the bowl. Somehow it will execute a ninety-degree turn, going somewhere completely different—usually onto a just-cleaned floor. Misdirection is bad enough. At other times, my pee stream splits into multiple personalities. Move over, Sybil. My pee stream can have well over sixteen different personalities. Each drop with a mind of its own. "I'm going to go *here*!" *I'm* going to go *there*!" Like Shirley Mason—the real Sybil who was faking it the whole time—I could give them names and fabricate histories. "Since I was abused, I'm not going to land in the bowl. I'm headed straight onto the seat, or better yet, the counter!" "My mother, the bladder, abandoned me when I was just a little drop of water. I'm going to stay right here in the penis where it's safe and warm. I'm not coming out at all. Fuck you, Frederick!"

Men, do your pee streams talk to you? What the hell are they trying to say? It wasn't always this way. Back in the day, my pee stream was strong and focused. It could do anything, go anywhere. It had drive! It had ambition! Eligible now for Medicare, I wouldn't even fix it up on a blind date. (Though drooling as it is, a literal blind date might in fact be the only one appropriate.) It's become such a risky proposition that I've taken to sitting down on the toilet, especially during the night. I guess this is why over thirty percent of Japanese men pee sitting down, and the worldwide movement to get men to do it this way, which has long been guided by Islamic culture, is growing.

As they say, aging ain't for sissies. It's also not for the humor-impaired. If you can't develop a sense of humor about your body breaking down, you're in for a really rough time. Take my prostate. Please. It must have swelled to the size of a football because it sure isn't letting much through the downfield goalposts.

And frequency? I have to pee after I pee. It's getting to the point where I'm afraid to leave the toilet because I know I'll have to pee again in a half hour. If I only get up three times a night to pee, it's a good night. Four or five times is more common. I would probably fix a suction tube to the head of my penis if I wasn't worried that it would fall off when I roll over in the night and present my girlfriend with a golden shower. Like the parent of a five-year-old, I ask myself if I have to pee before I go on a trip, even a ten-minute one to the store. When I land in some unfamiliar store or office, I immediately scope out where the nearest bathrooms are. I've peed in the back lots of countless restaurants, gas stations, and supermarkets because I couldn't wait for the bathroom to free up. I won't embarrass myself any further by talking about the times I haven't made it.

The top half of my long body has started the inevitable journey to reunite with the lower half. Gravity rules! Together, we're headed into the ground. Try as I might with yoga, neck rolls, and spinal stretching,

I've started to walk with a slight stoop. Like James Joyce's Mr. Duffy, I tend to reside a short distance from my body.

Knee-length compression socks are one of the hallmarks of aging. Had 'em for years. They're highly recommended for diabetics because the small veins in your feet tend to constrict and close over time. The socks keep blood circulation strong. What they're really good for is keeping the muscles in your arms and hands strong. They take such strength to get them over your heels and up your calf that you no longer have to lift weights.

"Man, you've got great biceps!"

"Yep, thanks to my compression socks."

The enamel on my teeth has had it. "We gave you sixty good years of bright white and now we're moving to the Ozarks." Stain, stain, stain. I'm lucky if I can last three months to make it back to the dentist before I start auditioning for movie parts featuring toothless, gumless, backwoods hillbillies. All those years of brushing and floss-ing … for what? Now I only have to inhale deeply at a coffee shop and my teeth turn brown. I don't even regularly drink coffee! I prefer tea. But I've given that up, too, because of the stains. My dentist thinks it's my Tibetan medicine—what I call "mudballs"—because the pills taste like dirt. She got me to grind the pills using a mortar and pestle. Now I pour hot water after I've crushed the pills and drink the sludge out of the mortar with a metal straw, sucking it directly into the back of my throat so it won't stain my front teeth. Does the Dalai Lama do this to keep his pearly whites?

Since stomach acid commonly attacks bone density, I suppose that's the culprit for my decomposing teeth. Acid reflux? I spend a good part of my day now coughing and belching because I feel like if I don't, I might vomit. I should invest in the company that owns Tums. All the foods I like to eat are jet fuel for the boiling cauldrons of cor-rosion in my stomach. Dairy, spices, sodas, alcohol, pizza, potato chips, burgers, and chocolate—the list goes on. You may ask, "What the hell is a sixty-seven-year-old man doing eating like a teenager anyway?!" Maybe acid reflux is a blessing in disguise to make me eat healthily. Given that the pH content of stomach acid is barely above that of battery acid, I could become a professional paint remover. I'll lick the walls clean. Couldn't make much difference to my digestive tract.

Severe back arthritis? I didn't even know you could get arthritis in your back. Is it from standing up too much? I thought arthritis was limited to your limbs. It's my torso and trunk—the very center and lower part of my chest. I might as well say, "My body is arthritis." That's what it feels like: in toto, the whole of it, top to bottom. When I get out of bed in the morning, sometimes it's a challenge to go vertical, to simply get erect. Stand up straight? Hell, I typically feel like I need to lie down again. Whoever thought bending over to tie my shoes might someday become a challenge? Crocs were made for people like me. Slip 'em on, slip 'em off—an arthritic's dream.

I blame my hearing challenges on short people. At six foot five (though dropping rapidly), I can't hear what people are saying at lower elevations. This problem is especially acute in public settings with a lot of background noise. I can't distinguish the background from the foreground. It all sounds like cacophony to me. It's not that I have hearing loss. My hearing is exceptionally good. In a sense, it's too good. I just can't separate out ancillary noises. Apparently, I have "cocktail party syndrome," an auditory discrimination problem known as central auditory processing disorder (CAPD.) Wonderful, yet another disorder. I bend over and lean in, trying to hear what a five-foot-tall person might be saying. Now I blame my stooping and height-loss problem on short people too.

TMJ? Sheesh. I can't even yawn in the morning anymore without getting my jaw stuck open. I recently asked my dentist what the next step would be if someday I can't get it closed. "Surgery," she said. That's it. That's all that lies between me and a look of perpetual open-mouthed wonder. Sign me up as a featured extra for a Steven Spielberg cutaway when a spaceship lands.

Don't get me started on toe fungus. I'll just say that if my diabetes gets so bad that they have to cut my foot off, I pray it's the foot with the toe fungus. That's the only thing that'll fix it. I'll donate my foot to the fungus. With my luck, once my foot is cut off, the fungus would die too and I'd get lawsuits from descendants of the "victim."

Heart Attacks and God

I've always been afraid of heart attacks. It must stem from my father's death when I was nine. But over the years, this fear has flowered into a life of its own.

I recently learned that more diabetics die of heart attacks than any other direct cause. Good to know. Now I can strike diabetes-induced kidney failure, stroke, blindness, and lethal infection off my fear list.

My fear was indirectly reinforced by Ram Dass. He long had fears of having a stroke and he mentioned it in his writings and public appearances. Yet his sharing of that as the ultimate manifestation of his demise did nothing to disrupt its eventual arrival. In 1997, the worst came to pass and he suffered a massive stroke.

I find that deeply discouraging. I tend to employ that as one of my operative life strategies. It works like this: If I speak a fear openly and freely acknowledge it in some way, then it will prevent the event from actually occurring. Call it reverse hubris. Or black humor with an agenda. Philosophically it goes like this: Who am I to presume to be so all-knowing and all-seeing that I can predict the future?

If I have the temerity to state a fear openly—"Hey, let's go to the Everglades this winter. Who knows if we'll both be *alive* next winter!"—then that genuflection to my own lack of omniscience will reap its own rewards, affirming that the likelihood is, in fact, I *will* still be alive next winter. More than that, I believe the odds of surviving until then will actually *increase* because, god knows, nothing ever works out in life as we mere mortals imagine and foresee. It's a way of disarming the demons of death by inviting them in. Like telling someone to break a leg before they head onstage. Reverse psychology.

I love the saying, "When humans make plans, God laughs." Within reason, I've tried to live by that understanding. But Ram Dass ruined it. Thanks, Ram Dass!

Nonetheless, I recognize this tool can be an adroit psychological move that has tangible benefits. Speak the fear, and by moving it from the unacknowledged to the acknowledged, it will release its hold. A lifetime of experience has proven to me that it can work.

Those more familiar with this sort of dynamic call it "bargaining with God" or "magical thinking." Like much of what I do in my life, I have to do everything backward. I can't make a simple, straightforward plea, "Please, God, don't let this happen." I preemptively say surely it *will* happen and throw down the gauntlet. "Go ahead, God, take my life. Show me what you got! I dare you!" Is this a Jewish cultural trait? It strikes me as one. It certainly takes chutzpah. I don't think reverse psychology would particularly impress the All-Seeing One: "It's that neurotic little SOB Marx again...tempting fate. Pretending he's going to die tomorrow. What the hell? Let's zap him with a lightning bolt this time just for laughs."

God and I have come a long way. I used to not believe in God. Well, I still don't. But now I believe in god. As a Jew, raised as an athe-ist, presently practicing Buddhism, that's no small admission.

God with a capital G connotes all things disagreeable to me about Judeo-Christian religions. The dogma. The history. The wars. The pol-itics. The hierarchies. The subjugation. The exploitation. The imagery. The White guy with the beard on the big throne. Guilt. Sin...I'm sorry, but to me, there's a lot of awful stuff there. To me, it signifies a deeply problematic worldview. For years, I would get triggered if the very word came up in conversation.

I didn't care which direction it came from. They were all abhorrent. Born again Christians, Muslims, Protestants, Methodists, Catholics, even Unitarians...I didn't care who spoke it. I just knew it could quickly become a diatribe directed at me. "Jews for Jesus" stand out in my mind. Of all the propagandists populating the quad on my hometown

University of Illinois' campus, which was full of them in the mid-1970s, they were the most obnoxious. I don't know why, but it seemed an inordinate number of them were filled by ranks of Jews from Skokie, Illinois, who I found wholly obnoxious to begin with, even before their conversion to Christianity. After that conversion? Holy God. The aggressiveness, the pigheadedness, the dogma, the rumpled clothes, the bad breath ... It was a toxic cocktail.

But god with a lowercase g is acceptable to me as a kind of short-hand. What it means to me is something like this ... Wait for it ... The way things happen. Ta-da! Yes, god is reality. You could say I think "god" is "everything." No limits in time and space. The all-inclusive daily special. Every action, every place, every occurrence—"god" is everywhere and everything. Of course, if you look at it philosophically, (or cynically), you could argue that it's another way of saying "god" is "nothing." If it's everything everywhere that ever happens, then it has no distinguishing features and cannot be described as anything other than the totality of the way things are. There's no self-standing articulation, no sep-arateness. But I don't accept that means it's meaningless. It means something—many things, in fact—to me. It's "the universe"; it's "all that exists"; it's "the mystery"; it's "the one"; it's "spirit"; it's "the eternal pres-ent." It's vague; I admit it. But I'm only comfortable with the term when it's nontheistic. It suggests that though there may be an animating con-sciousness in all that occurs, infused *within* all of life, (though not, in my view, "behind" or "directing" all life), we can never know it. It also sug-gests that there is meaning in life and that one can find it everywhere; it just may not be the meaning we think we already know or actively seek. It suggests that there is unity in multiplicity. That would mean that all religions are equally valid renderings of this thing called "god." It sug-gests that there is an uncertain, unpredictable perfection all around us in everything that occurs and that our task lies in perceiving it. We only need to let go of our strong desire that things should be otherwise.

The fact that we live in a quantum universe where a particle and a wave can be simultaneously there and not there makes things even more interesting. Reality is not some fixed, boring thing. It's constantly in flux, morphing and changing into new forms—many of which do not observe the laws of Newtonian physics—like the altered states commonly associated with psychedelics. It may well include past life emanations, teleportation, transubstantiation, dream manifestation, psychokinesis, and forms of life after death. That said, I don't need phantasmagoria to see god in everything and everyone. I find real everyday life endlessly enthralling. I seem to have gotten over being a drama queen. Or maybe now I just find drama in smaller places.

Despite its vagueness, "god" can be meaningful and even instructive when used to connote this abstraction of oneness. Call it the kinder, gentler abstraction. Though it contains room within it for the fireworks of hellfire and damnation like those in the Old Testament, it's bigger—even bigger than the New Testament.

But it has tremendous practical value. Using "god" in daily conversation can be helpful because it can be used interchangeably when others use "God." When you speak, nobody knows which letters are capitalized.

For someone like me—again, a Jewish-atheist-Buddhist, and life-long leftist—it's amazing how much the word shows up in everyday conversation with friends, in men's circles, in meditation meetings, and filmmaking. I don't cringe when I hear it anymore. My occasional uses of it help expedite communication. And they establish connections with other people. I'd rather build bridges than walls, at least when I'm not craving burning them down.

On a working visit to Iran in 2004, I delighted in conversations about "God" with friends. When my young colleague, Neda, told me how she was working very hard, neglecting sleep, meals, and exercise, I confidently told her that "god" wanted her to take better care of herself. I was playing it both ways. To myself, I was saying "god." But I knew she would, and did, hear "God." Like her family and pretty much everyone in the country, she was devoutly Muslim. For me, it's become a practiced little deception, like making a promise with fingers crossed. "God" or "god"—I make them interchangeable.

I no longer suffer through having to explain my view of the cosmos and my use of "god" over "God." It's a line of reasoning that's never succinctly summarized. I still do it when necessary, but I loathe reconstructing this explanation in daily conversation. Now that I use "god" and "God" interchangeably, I don't wrinkle my nose and shrug or make air quotes with my fingers like I used to. Communicating with mainstream folks the world over has become so much easier. I save a lot of time and energy by saying "god," while letting others assume I mean "God." At least I think that's what they assume. But maybe I'm the mistaken one. Perhaps when they use "God," they're really saying "god." Who knows? I'm afraid to ask. God only knows.

A Boy Named Rakasu

CONVENTION OF THE HAIRLESS

From left to right: Junpo Denis Kelly, Fugen Tom Pitner,
Frederick Marx
[photo by Holly Million]

(A *rakasu* is a traditional Japanese garment, like a bib, worn around
the neck of Zen Buddhists who have taken the precepts. It can also
signify Lay Ordination.)

Look out, world. I've been ordained as a Zen Priest! January 12,
2017, a day that will live in infamy!

I'm not entirely comfortable with the term "priest." I prefer "Zen Dude." (My motto? "The Priest Abides.") The mission statement of our Hollow Bones Order? *We are a sacred order, bringing into being a harmonious and loving world, through the practice of meditative, compassionate awareness and mindful stewardship.*

What happens during a Zen ordination ceremony? Much finery and protocol, a lot of bowing, chanting, taking of vows, and Zen being Zen, lots of spontaneity and ribald humor.

Photo by William Prince

The photo above shows my teacher, Junpo, applying soap before shaving the last little tuft of hair off the back of my head. The baldness—symbolic of our rebirth into a new, awakened life—is designed to remind us of our vows and keep us humble. Since I'm shocked every time I look in the mirror, I'd say it's working. Always needing to wear a cap to counter the freezing cold also helps.

In the first part of the ceremony, I enter wearing only a white robe, signifying the seeker's purity of purpose. Underneath that, I had on only underpants. Not being naturally adept at elaborate body movements, much less at wearing finery, I kept wondering how Junpo was dealing with me unintentionally flashing him. If he noticed, he maintained a straight face. "Ah, Grasshopper flashing Master. Too bad for Master!" Junpo being Junpo, he did point out that my shaved face and pate would soon become a female magnet once I added an earring, which for him, was de rigueur. Complete projection, no doubt. I confessed that my first thought on committing to a minimum of one year of hairlessness was how it would affect my dating life.

Next to me is Kisen Lynn Bosche, who chose to do the ceremony without all the finery. I respect that choice since I myself thought at one time that I might replicate what the Buddha did, compositing my robe out of discarded rags. But I knew the greater challenge for me was, and always will be, to care for and wear the highly elaborate traditional regalia. Talk about comedy. Just ask me not to trip or tear anything doing full prostrations.

You might note my friend and mentor, Fugen Tom Pitner, standing behind me with a huge razor-sharp sword. This being *Rinzai* Zen, the chosen Buddhist practice of Japanese samurai, Fugen is obliged to cut off my head if he senses any hint of wavering in my commitment. Let's just say that I responded very enthusiastically to every question so he didn't have to wrestle with any drastic decisions.

Arriving at this moment had been my clear intention since I finished my previous Hollow Bones retreat a year prior. I realized then that if I truly wanted to move past a life of neurosis, I had to dedicate myself to living in Zen Mind. I certainly couldn't have known it then, but my stepped-up practice over that year proved immense in supporting me through the dying and death of my wife and the tremendous grief that followed.

But I saw myself functioning like a minister in the world long before I officially attained the moniker. For the previous three to four years, I had a Post-It Note over my desk that read: "It's about your Ministry, not your <u>Career</u>!" I was evolving into some kind of spiritual or thought leader long before I knew what kind.

Ever since I was a teen, I have been drawn to the dharma. At fifteen, I found *The Book* by Alan Watts in our house and devoured it. I read *Be Here Now* by Ram Dass a few years later. I wanted to study and practice Buddhism from those early beginnings but had nowhere to turn in my little East Central Illinois prairie town to follow up. I didn't know it at the time, but I wanted to take refuge. "Taking refuge" is the term we use for committing to the Buddhist path. Specifically, we take refuge in the "Three Jewels."

1. The Buddha: the model that Siddhartha Gautama provided with his life, waking us to life's hard realities and pointing the way to enlightenment;
2. The Dharma: the teachings themselves, the truth about how life is best lived to minimize suffering and maximize peace and fulfillment;
3. The Sangha: the community of fellow practitioners who support each other through the trials of learning and growth.

All three elements are essential to support the path of awakening. Life is hard and full of pain and loss. So, taking refuge is both figurative and real. This is how we word the "Three Refuge" vows we take in Hollow Bones:

1. I take refuge in the absolute purity of this awakened mind (Buddha).
2. I take refuge in this practice of pure awareness, wisdom, compassion, and skillful means (Dharma).
3. I take refuge in this awakening community, and our realization in the truth of the interconnection, interpenetration, and interdependency of all sentient and insentient beings (Sangha).

Even better known than the Three Refuges is the Bodhisattva Vow, which takes different forms in different Buddhist traditions. I used a version of the Bodhisattva Vow to open my film *Journey from Zanskar,* adapting the text from more traditional phrasings to best fit the film's narrative: "Though beings are innumerable, I vow to free them from all suffering." All the different versions of Bodhisattva Vows express fundamental paradoxes. The four "Awakened One's" vows I took for my Hollow Bones ordination no less so:

- *However innumerable all beings are, I vow to serve and liberate them all.*
- *However deep and elusive my shadow states are, I vow to experience and enlighten them all.*
- *However vast and difficult true teachings are, I vow to embody and master them all.*
- *However endless my true path may be, I vow to awaken and follow forever.*

There are some unique features to those vows. Certainly, the emphasis on "shadow" is wholly uncharacteristic of most Buddhist traditions. Typically, "delusion" or "ignorance" is used. In Hollow Bones, we implicitly acknowledge that every human being carries "shadows." We must root out all unconscious expressions of shadow before we can truly mature as human beings, much less reach the non-dual state of enlightenment. That means we must turn and face all that we typically hide, repress, and deny about ourselves. We can't bypass our human conditioning.

We also emphasize embodiment. This human body is our only vehicle for awakening. It cannot be discounted or bypassed on the path to realization. It must be cared for, exercised, well-maintained, and properly nourished. Flossing may not directly lead to enlightenment, but it will certainly help maintain the body that makes enlightenment possible.

What does one actually do when one becomes a Zen Dude? For me, that question became real late that fall. Before then, I was only clear that I needed to pursue the path for selfish reasons. I wanted once and for all to stop identifying with my own neuroses. I'd had it. I was tired of self-created suffering.

"What does being ordained signify?" people started to ask me. Once ordained, some people become monks and continue to deepen their study and practice in monasteries. Not for me, thank you. Others found Buddhist churches, building flocks and becoming local institutions. That also doesn't speak to me. I don't want to build an institution. My own small filmmaking nonprofit is headache enough, thank you. What options does this leave? One thing I know is I want to dedicate the good works of the remainder of my life to the memory of my departed wife. I'm still sorting out the rest, but here's some of what I know …

I'd like to give public dharma talks. There is so much suffering everywhere, especially since Covid and Collapse. I want to hang out the proverbial shingle and see if anyone shows up. "Suffering? Got the blues? Here's a free talk that might help …."

I had a surprising, largely inexplicable vision during a workshop I took in December before my ordination. I'd like to host a podcast called *Life with Zen Dude*—a cross between Dr. Phil and Stephen Colbert with a focus on dharma. We'll no doubt start on the web and likely never appear elsewhere. I want to have everyday people (perhaps with occasional experts or celebrities) talk about their life challenges in emotional and authentic ways.

I'll offer them all the support I can from twenty-seven years of men's work, thirty-five years of dharma study and practice, and a lifetime of experience. I'll aim to make it by turns playful and fun, as well as helpful and practical for all those watching. Though it's a connection never consciously intended by me, it's safe to say this book is a first step.

Meanwhile, you'll see me hanging out in Beginner's Mind. Getting nowhere…

Photo by William Prince

Becoming Nobody

I always wanted to be somebody. That was my first mistake. I was in trouble from the start. Worse, I've repeated it. Throughout my life, I've persisted in trying to be somebody.

I've now repeated that mistake thousands of times. It's safe to say I'll never learn—doing the same thing, expecting different results. Yes, that is the commonly held definition of mental illness.

I recently watched *Becoming Nobody* featuring Ram Dass, my lifetime hero. Famous back in the early 1960s as Timothy Leary's partner at Harvard, he conducted experiments using LSD, psilocybin, and other hallucinogens and became somebody at an early age. He was known as Richard Alpert back then. In 1967, he traveled to India and met his lifetime guru, Neem Karoli Baba, who gave him the name Ram Dass—servant of Ram (a.k.a. servant of God). He then spent the next fifty years of his life doing just that by writing books, giving talks, and setting up nonprofits, while becoming more and more famous and beloved. Not bad! No servant on *Downton Abbey* succeeded like that.

The someone journey has been a bit of a bell curve for me. Though I had rising success in my twenties and thirties, I was largely still a nobody. Then at thirty-nine, I suddenly became somebody through *Hoop Dreams*. My proverbial fifteen minutes of fame lasted over two years. It was quite the run! I had Academy and Emmy Award nominations, international film festivals and awards, press interviews, and keynote speeches. I got an agent and had regular meetings in Hollywood. Then it all nosedived. Other than a few perks and privileges here and there, my fame factor returned close to zero and largely stayed there for the next twenty-five years despite making ten films and writing three books. That side of the graph is less like a bell curve and more like falling off a cliff; I landed hard on the rocks and stayed there. The whole journey in a nutshell? I was a nobody who became somebody, then returned to being a nobody again. Like Marlon Brando lamenting to his older brother Rod Steiger in *On the Waterfront*, too often I find myself moaning, "I coulda been someone. I coulda been a contender."

For years, I've wondered, "If a film screens in a forest and no one is there to see it, does it make a sound?" Getting films funded is bad enough, but now getting them seen is proving impossible. Given those struggles, I resolved to turn my life into an art object. It's the cheapest canvas around and, except when you're home alone, you pretty much have an audience all the time. Best of all, though it helps to pay for a few workshops here and there and read a few self-help books, typically you don't have to go out and fundraise. Of course, any signs of success become even more ephemeral than writing a book or making a movie, but you can still create whenever you want for as long as you want. You can create 'til you die!

That's all in the outward sense of society's standard measurements of achievement and success. Becoming nobody is ultimately an inside job. It's about losing any attachment to any particular way of being, even of being a work of art yourself, giving up any expectations of outcomes, and becoming agnostic about needs. Most people would call it becoming egoless. Ram Dass eventually discovered that his identity as a spiritual guru was just as confining as his former identity as a Harvard academic. When he showed up, people expected the Ram Dass show—kindness, wisdom, and the whole spiritual parade. For a while, he tried being his pissy "natural" self, but that failed too. That, too, felt performative. He tried hard to become nobody and felt like he failed.

For me, that inward journey flatlined from beginning to end. I never left the rocks. I started with ego, got my ego affirmed, and lived with ego ever since. I'll probably die with ego, checking my IMDB ranking with my last breath. It seems I'll never rise to the higher standard of true selflessness; it feels like the Holy Grail. I've been somebody all along—a strange ego identification with this bag of aging bones called Frederick Marx—and I despair of ever changing. Like the peasant crying out at the end of Part 1 of Bertolucci's masterpiece *1900*, "Where is socialism?!" you might someday recognize my plaintive cry, "Where is nobody?!"

I've returned again to a familiar decision point: Do I want to spend the rest of my life in "woulda, coulda, shoulda" mode, attached to this ephemera called self, telling myself over and over again a story about who I am—"A Loser!"—or would I like to become nobody and be happy? You'd think it'd be an easy choice, but attachment is fierce, even to a sinking ship. Egos typically do not willingly deconstruct.

I'm reminded of an aphorism from Chögyam Trungpa Rinpoche: "The bad news is you're falling through the air, nothing to hang on to, no parachute. The good news is there's no ground." But this doesn't stop us from reaching out to try and grab on to stuff, does it? Even if they're broken branches and razor-sharp rocks—metaphors for all the wounds and losses we've suffered—we're desperate for something to hold on to. The stories we tell ourselves—this is who I am, this shall not change—are the hardest and last to go. "I am these losses. I am these wounds." Not remotely factual, but an illusion with great attraction.

For years, I kept asking myself if I was doing the right thing with my life. Surely, it would've been easier to be something other than a filmmaker. Maybe I was really supposed to drive a cab, wait tables, or deliver mail? But all this time, I've been asking myself the wrong question. Instead of, "What am I supposed to be doing with my life?" It should have been, "What am I doing so attached to the outcomes of my life?" I know what I'm here for. I'm supposed to be making films and writing books. It's a truth I know in my bones. It's just that living your soul's purpose bears no relation to outcomes. Just because you know you're doing what you're supposed to be doing doesn't mean anyone will give a shit. It all comes down to acceptance. Can I make peace with that?

For years, I thought my work might be discovered after I die. Nobody seems to appreciate artists as much as when they're dead. I've instructed my heirs to do everything possible to maximize any publicity from my death to promote and sell my work. Is this a vain attempt to extend ego beyond the grave? Perhaps. Most likely, I'll remain just as unknown dead as I am alive.

Is it possible to become somebody and nobody at the same time? Strive to achieve that external fame and recognition while being completely unattached to that as an outcome? Ram Dass never seemed to strive for success, yet he seemed to master that tightrope walk. The more he became somebody, the more he became nobody. I think that's what I'll aim for. It's certainly worth a try. Of course, with my luck, things will go horribly awry and I'll end up becoming everybody.

Thank You for Reading My Book

I hope you've appreciated *Turds of Wisdom*. It was a labor of love to condense so much of my life experience into one book. Before you go and start slinging around what you've digested, I have a small favor to ask:

Could you please write an Amazon review? Even if it's only one or two sentences, your review would mean a lot.

Simply go to this book's Amazon page, scroll down, and click "Write a customer review." Even if you did not buy the book from Amazon, you can still leave a review there.

Reviews are the best way for a "small" book like this one to get noticed and reach a wider audience. For this reason, your support really does make a difference.

Thanks again for reading. I wish you much success in your journey, especially now that you can drop a few Turds of Wisdom on your friends and family!

Sincerely,
Frederick Marx

Acknowledgments

First, I want to thank all the advance readers of my book. Making your way through a comedy book that isn't funny is not easy. Secondly, I want to thank everyone I've ever met. You've made my life pretty funny.

Bows to my old China friend Alan Atkinson for checking up on my Chinese colloquialisms. Ryan Cove did far more than any copy editor can reasonably be expected to do, suggesting abundant and productive structural, editorial, and even title changes. Though I've lost Austin Pierce to far more lucrative and meaningful life tasks than marketing my books, his instincts proved impeccable yet again when he suggested final title and subtitle changes. My esteemed men's work colleague Jed Diamond led me to Bill Gladstone at Waterside Productions and my first official publishing deal. Thank you for that. Further bows to Stu Selland and Stephanie Dewey for wrestling the photos into usable shape.

The expression "the love of my life" is overused. I all too often revert to cliches myself, but I have to acknowledge my girlfriend Maggie and what bounty she delivers to my life. She offered much practical assistance editing photos, reviewing drafts, and tweaking graphics. From a mysterious source beyond nature, she embodies the life force itself, capable of bringing the dying bounding to their feet. She certainly did that for me. With inexhaustible love, caring, compassion, and humor, she, more than anything or anyone, inspires me to plod on.

Made in United States
Orlando, FL
16 April 2023

32153846R00086